BECOMING WHOLE

BECOMING WHOLE

A Journey of Identity, Theology, Liberation, and the God Who Holds It All

AmunDayo Khepra Oloririi Edwards

Foreword by Edward Donalson III

RESOURCE *Publications* · Eugene, Oregon

BECOMING WHOLE
A Journey of Identity, Theology, Liberation, and the God Who Holds It All

Resource Publications
An Imprint of Wipf and Stock Publishers
199 W. 8th Ave., Suite 3
Eugene, OR 97401

www.wipfandstock.com

PAPERBACK ISBN: 979-8-3852-6655-5
HARDCOVER ISBN: 979-8-3852-6656-2
EBOOK ISBN: 979-8-3852-6657-9

VERSION NUMBER 02/26/26

IN MEMORIAM

In Loving Memory of Bobbie Jean Baker
Your life was a sermon of resilience, grace, and divine authenticity.
You showed us that holiness could dance, that healing could sing,
and that God's image is big enough to hold every part of who we are.
Your courage carved space for so many of us to breathe—
to live fully, freely, and unapologetically.
Though your earthly song has ended, your spirit continues to move
through our rhythms of resistance and praise.
You remind me still: becoming whole is not about erasing our story,
but embodying it with love.

In Loving Memory of My Grandmother, Lydia Eleece Hayes-Simpson
You did more than pass down your name; you passed down your *anointing.*
Your prayers became the roots of my strength,
your laughter, the music of my calling,
and your wisdom, the compass of my soul.
You walked between worlds with grace—
anchored in faith, guided by Spirit, and alive with ancestral knowing.
Through you, I inherited not only legacy but *lineage*:
a current of spiritual power that continues to move through my hands,
my voice, my ministry, and my becoming.
Your love still speaks through the silence,
and your energy reminds me that ancestry is eternity in motion.

In Loving Memory of My Godparents, Rickey and Madelynn Tates
Your unconditional love continues to carry me forward.
You nurtured me with compassion, guided me with truth,
and loved me with the kind of faith that cannot be forgotten.

Even beyond this realm, your spiritual visitations remind me
of a connection that moves beyond time and space—
a holy communion that transcends the veil.
Thank you for teaching me that presence is not limited to the body,
and that love—real love—never stops showing up.

In Loving Memory of My Other Mama, Janice Sommerville

You believed in me when I was still learning how to believe in myself.
Your encouragement pushed me toward my goals
and became a wind beneath my ministry's wings.
You saw what I could not yet see—
that the call on my life was not a burden but a blessing.
Because of you, I learned that faith can look like patience,
that love can sound like accountability,
and that support can be the soil where calling takes root.
Your legacy is not only in what you gave me,
but in how you taught me to give myself—freely, courageously, and with purpose.

Each of you have become a part of the divine echo that guides my journey. Your love is my inheritance; your memory, my map. May these words honor the ways you shaped my becoming—in life, in spirit, and in every breath of this work.

DEDICATION

To my parents, Gerald Edwards and Joan Parker,
who gave me life, faith, and the first language of love.
To my brothers, Detrick (DL), and Damond, (D-Money),
who taught me strength through laughter and survival.
To my aunt, Gwen Eaton,
whose wisdom steadied me when the world felt uncertain,
and my sister-cousin, Courtney Smith—your love and faith in
me have been a steady flame in seasons of darkness.
To my children, Correen, Sheldon, Howard, Sajian & Marjha,
Leon and Dykiesha (Kiki), Taliyah, Imani and LeAnthony
(L.A), and Malcolm, who remind me every day what
redemption looks like in motion.
To my church community,
Integrated Praise Spiritual Center (IPSC), whose prayers,
songs, and sacred questions have kept my heart tethered to hope.
And last but never least—
To the love of my life, my best friend, my wife,
Anés-a Ànyánwá, (Christine Campbell-Edwards) whose
presence reminds me that love is the purest form of worship.
You are my mirror, my melody,
and the living proof that God is love made visible.
This book is for you all—
for every hand that has held me,
every voice that has believed in me,
and every heart that continues to walk beside me
on this journey of becoming whole.

"So God created humankind in the divine image;
in the image of God they were created."

— *Genesis 1:27 (NRSV)*

Contents

Foreword

In times of authoritarianism, stories are an important way to inspire liberation movements. We are living in a historic moment globally when plutocrats and oligarchs are pushing societies toward a post-human intergalactic technocracy rooted in perverted, overt eugenics. One of the first stops toward universal domination is the total marginalization of people groups who are deemed transgressive or subversive. Those who find themselves with their backs perpetually against the wall are under direct attack from governments across the globe. This current global shift to the far right has focused its cruelest intentions on people of Trans experience because they represent a zone of possibility beyond binary thinking. Our siblings of Trans experience point toward liberation from traditional gender roles, but more than that, they challenge the patriarchy that upholds systems of power and domination.

For many, the drudgery of the quotidian has demolished every thought of what is possible outside the harsh realities of fear and violence that govern their existence. All hope of liberation escapes those who live in a world ruled by systems of domination and face the burden of multiple marginalizations. The soul-crushing realities of everydayness for millions of people who do not fit the standards of normativity dictated in the United States of America by a relatively small number of people, but held in a majoritarian ideation, make for a minoritarian life of terror. Black people, disabled people, people experiencing the effects of poverty, LGBTQIA+ people, female embodied people, and so many more identities who share space in the realm of the radical "other" are constantly looking to the elsewhere, otherwise, and elsewhen for the hope of escape from what Frantz Fanon called the zone of nonbeing.

In this work, Rev. AmunDayo Edwards shares the story of his journey to wholeness. He invites us to see the triumph of resistance. We are reminded that the most revolutionary act in this world is daring to be yourself. When you dare to imagine a world of authenticity in the face of domination, you have become the epitome of velour. In revealing the journey of his own becoming, we are invited to become. Whether you are on a gender journey or other types of becoming this work shares tools for resisting the soul crushing reality of systems of domination that seek to create cookie-cutter compliant people who fear their own potential. This is a story of authenticity with the power to release the authenticity in every reader.

While right-wing evangelical white nationalist dominate the narrative of the Christian faith in the media, there has always been a prophetic impulse found among those most impacted by social structures designed to ensure their subjugation and the power status of the ruling elite. Increasingly, people are becoming aware that the society born of systemic oppression will never provide liberty or justice to most of those who comprise that society. When the gifts of radical love are unlocked by the minoritarian, both the minoritarian and majoritarian are saved. AmunDayo offers a glimpse of the radical love of Jesus as a pastor in the Christian tradition. He shows in this work the antithesis of the hate-filled rhetoric that has hijacked the evangelical world. While the media fixation has amplified voices of Christo-fascism in the pages of this book, there is a revelation of a pure faith in Divine love.

As we journey through this hinge time where the realities of imperialist capitalist anti-Black cisheteropatriarchy are unmasked in ways the person thought were indicators of by gone eras, the need for prophetic voices is clear. The temptation is to believe the prophet shows the folly of the powerful and not the full picture of complicity with power. However, showing where the folly of power leads is only the beginning of the task of the prophet; a cultural critic can do that work without prophetic impulse. The prophetic impulse is not satiated in mystical encounters with the Divine; the fulfillment of the prophetic impulse is the return to community, where praxis is engaged. Prophetic traditions aim to transform the world in in such a way that the beloved community is posed to birth new worlds of justice. Prophetic voices seek to paint a new world with the toolkit of oral performance, imagination, and keen intellectual investigation so that the hearer is left with a picture of a preferable future. The prophetic task of the modern prophet is not merely to predict an outcome, but rather to identify concrete evils.

Writing one's story is a courageous act of self-disclosure, and more importantly for our reading of this work, it gives a resistant voice to the terrorist efforts of colonial erasure. As a ministerial gift, Pastor Edwards calls all people to refuse the fascist impulses that seek to thingify the human experience while cloaking themselves diabolically in the name of Christianity. Hope built on testimony leads to triumphant overcoming. In this text, AmunDayo Edwards, in the tradition of the late Minister Bobby Jean Baker and Miss Majors, pours his life out on these pages as the Blood of the Lamb, which indeed becomes the Word of our collective testimony. There is in the pages of this book, the altar upon which our own stories can become a sweet-smelling savor.

There is in the words of these pages a narrative of redemption, but more than that the beginning of a blueprint to liberation. In the lines of personal story the universal is revealed in ways that call forth the power of the individual. Find your power in the strength and resilience of a life lived toward and in the service of truth. Find your grief, joy, and voice in the telling of events you were not present for but make plain the experiences of your past. AmunDayo Edwards is a prophet for our times, speaking our deliverance into being. Calling forth the best of our humanity and spiritually by sharing his story, his journey, his truth! I pray that as you read the words of this book, you will find the strength and courage to live authentically and in doing so challenge all that seeks to truncate your person.

Dr. Edward Donalson III

Preface

There are some stories that refuse to stay silent. They live in the body, humming beneath the skin, waiting for the right season to speak. *Becoming Whole* is one of those stories.

For years, I carried these memories, questions, and revelations in fragments—journal entries, sermons, and reflections scribbled on napkins and prayer cards. I wrote in the margins of life, between pastoral duties, community work, and the quiet wrestling of identity. I didn't realize then that all those fragments were pieces of the same truth: a testimony about loss and liberation, about the faith that breaks you open and the God who puts you back together.

This book began to take form during a season of unraveling. Everything that had once defined me—ministry, relationships, certainty, even health—was shifting beneath my feet. I had built my life around holding things together, but the Spirit was calling me to let them fall apart. What I once called failure, I later recognized as formation. The breaking wasn't punishment; it was preparation.

I wrote through nights of silence that felt like judgment, through days when I questioned my own worth, and through moments when hope was as thin as breath. But somewhere in the midst of it, I began to feel God differently—not as the distant ruler I had been taught to fear, but as the indwelling presence I could not escape. God was not watching me suffer from afar. God was in the suffering, in the stillness, in the slow reconstruction of my soul.

Every chapter of this book carries some part of that process. It holds the echoes of the church that raised me, the ancestral rhythms that sustain me, and the metaphysical truths that set me free. I write as one shaped by the Black church's fire and discipline, yet also by the whispers of the ancestors, the songs of the earth, and the voice of Spirit that transcends all language. My theology is not bound by dogma—it is born of experience, dialogue, and discovery.

I did not set out to write a book of answers. I wrote as a witness. As someone who has been undone by pain and remade by grace. As someone who has been exiled from belonging and yet found home within. *Becoming Whole* is an invitation to explore the spaces between faith and freedom, memory and revelation, identity and divinity.

This work is also a reflection of my ministry. As a pastor and spiritual leader, I have seen the ways people carry invisible wounds—spiritual injuries that traditional theology often fails to name. We talk about sin but rarely about shame. We preach redemption but often ignore repair. Through my own healing journey, I began to understand that liberation is not just external, it is interior. It's what happens when we reclaim our story from the systems that told us who we weren't.

The timing of this book is not accidental. It comes at a moment when so many of us are being asked to return to ourselves—to remember what we've forgotten, to release what no longer serves, and to rise into who we truly are. Writing this was an act of remembrance and resistance, a way of saying to myself and to the world: *I am still here. And I am still becoming.*

For those who have ever been told that your voice is too loud, your love too unconventional, your body too complicated, or your faith too expansive—this book is for you. For those who have felt unseen by the Church but never unloved by God, for those who have struggled to hold faith and freedom in the same breath, and for those who are still piecing themselves together one truth at a time—this book is for you, too.

May these words remind you that your story is sacred, your questions are holy, and your becoming is not a detour—it is divine design. May you find in these pages what I found in the writing: permission to be fully human and profoundly whole.

Because wholeness is not perfection. It is permission. Permission to exist as you are. Permission to love as you are. Permission to believe, to doubt, to rise, and to rest in the knowing that the God who holds the world together is holding you.

AmunDayo Khepra Oloririi

Acknowledgments

WRITING THIS BOOK HAS been a journey of surrender, healing, and revelation. I am deeply grateful to every person, seen and unseen, who has walked beside me on the path of becoming.

To my parents, whose love and imperfections both shaped and stretched me. You gave me roots strong enough to withstand the storm and wings brave enough to search for home.

To my brothers, whose laughter kept me grounded in the realness of family. To my aunt, whose wisdom whispered truth into moments of confusion.

To my entire family—the *Hayes, Edwards, Harris, Eaton, and Riley* clans, thank you for loving me through every season of becoming. Your prayers, laughter, and unwavering support have been the steady ground beneath my feet. Each of you, in your own way, helped me grow into the person I was always meant to be.

To my church community, the people of *Integrated Praise Spiritual Center*, you are my spiritual family, my sacred classroom, and my living testimony that love can build what religion once broke.

To *Pastor Doretha Williams-Flournoy*, my forever pastor, and the *A Church For All* family, I began my rediscovery of myself while serving with you. We held our first services with your blessing and support, and from that sacred beginning, a mighty movement was born. Thank you for teaching me how to be a great leader. Your legacy lives on in me.

To *Dr. Yvette Flunder* and *The Fellowship of Affirming Ministries*, thank you for helping me walk fully into my being. Through your ministry, I saw what was possible. As I served as Regional Minister and Co-Facilitator for TransSaints — a ministry created to provide support, education, fellowship, and resources for all people of trans experience and affirming churches — my own walk toward freedom became the very process that shaped me into the man I am today.

To *Queen Mother MaShiAat Oloya Tyehimba-Ford*, who introduced me to a part of myself I had not yet met—my Indigenous lineage. You opened my eyes to more than I could have ever seen on my own, and in doing so, you not only gave me a name but a purpose.

To my Bishop and friend, *Dr. Edward Donalson, III (Oluyemi Oladeji Kalimara),* thank you for your covering, counsel, and the generous way you continue to affirm my calling. Your wisdom and voice echo through these pages, and your contribution to this work through the *Foreword* is a gift of spiritual lineage and love.

To my editor, *Rev. Dr. Doris Cope*, (mama Cope) thank you for your patience, your sensitivity, and your eye for both language and spirit. You honored the rhythm of my story while helping it breathe with greater clarity.

To my friends and colleagues in ministry and community, thank you for the countless prayers, check-ins, and gentle reminders to rest.

And finally, to the love of my life, my best friend, and my wife, *Anés-a Ànyánwá,* (Christine Campbell-Edwards) you have held space for my transformation with grace and courage. You remind me every day that love is both sanctuary and mirror. You have loved me through and beyond my pain; you have seen me for who I am, not who I once believed myself to be, and you have stood by me even when I didn't make it easy. You are my calm in the storm, my light in the darkness, and my iron that sharpens iron. I am better, stronger, and greater because you stand with me. I love you deeply and will forever be grateful for your unwavering, unconditional love and devotion.

This book was born from the labor of many hearts-human and divine. To the ancestors who carried me through silence, to Spirit who kept whispering, and to every reader who dares to become—thank you. May these words remind you that you are never beyond redemption, never outside of love, and never finished becoming whole.

Introduction

I HAVE SPENT MOST of my life searching—searching for love, for truth, for freedom, for God, and for myself. What began as a child's quiet longing to be seen and held became an adult's quest to understand the sacred pattern behind every wound, every awakening, every return to my truest self.

This book is born from that search. It is not a memoir in the traditional sense, though my story runs through every page. It is not strictly theology, though I wrestle with God in every chapter. *Becoming Whole* is a spiritual excavation—a journey through memory, identity, and belief—toward a deeper knowing of the God who holds it all.

I come to this work as one shaped by the fire and the silence. The fire taught me endurance, the way trial can purify without consuming, the way struggle can carve room for Spirit. The silence taught me to listen—to hear the voice of God beneath the noise, to rest in the spaces where no music plays, where healing hums in stillness.

I was raised in the sound and structure of the Black church—where tambourines testified, and voices carried the prayers of generations. I learned early that the Spirit could move through rhythm, through sound, through breath—that freedom could find its way through the clap of hands and the cry of "Hallelujah." In the Black church tradition, *shouting* is more than noise; it is a sacred, embodied response to the Holy Spirit—a dance, a cry, a release that turns pain into power and worship into survival.

Yet I also came to know that not all who shouted were free. Some of us were shouting to keep from breaking, shouting to drown out the silence that reminded us of our pain. The shout was our survival, the silence our sanctum. Between the two, I learned that liberation is not always loud—it can be a quiet returning, a steady breath, a whisper that says, *I'm still here.*

Faith, for me, has always been a kind of inheritance and interrogation. I inherited a God of miracles and mercy, but also of rules and restraint. I inherited joy, but I also inherited silence—the kind that keeps you from asking questions, the kind that confuses obedience with holiness. Over time, those questions I wasn't allowed to ask became the ones that guided me back to God in a new way.

The sacred story of *Becoming Whole* began when the structures that once defined my faith began to collapse. The God I had been handed could no longer hold the complexity of my humanity. I needed a God big enough for my Blackness, my queerness, my tenderness, my truth. And so began the work of unlearning and remembering, of sifting through the rubble of religion to find the living Spirit still breathing underneath it all.

My path has wound through the pews of Pentecostal fire, the silence of metaphysical awakening, and the ancestral wisdom of Indigenous and African cosmologies. Each encounter taught me something about the divine—how Spirit moves through all things, how the ancestors whisper through wind and water, how healing is both a personal act and a collective responsibility. I have learned that truth does not belong to one language, one religion, or one revelation. The Holy meets us wherever we are willing to be honest. And sometimes honesty sounds like doubt, feels like grief, or looks like freedom.

This book is my testimony to that truth. It is about the long road between survival and surrender, between faith inherited and faith discovered. It is about what happens when the soul refuses to stay silent in the face of contradiction.

For many of us, faith was shaped in systems that told us who we had to be—what holiness looked like, how love should sound, and who could belong. I believed those rules for a long time, until the walls of certainty could no longer contain my becoming. Pain broke me open, but Spirit met me there—in the breaking. That's where I began to understand that holiness isn't perfection; it's honesty.

Liberation, I've come to learn, is not only external—it's internal. It's the moment you realize that God was never outside of you, waiting for you to measure up, but within you, waiting for you to wake up. Theologians call it incarnation. Mystics call it union. I call it coming home.

Throughout these pages, I reflect on the sacred intersections of theology and lived experience—where scripture meets story, and where the divine meets the human. I explore what it means to heal the fractured parts of self: the child who was silenced, the believer who felt unworthy, the seeker who longed to be free. In that healing, I discovered a God who is not either/or, but *both/and*—both transcendent and immanent, both Father and Mother, both Spirit and Flesh, both ancient and ever-new.

To be whole, I learned, is not to erase our contradictions but to integrate them. Wholeness is what happens when we stop running from our shadow and start listening to what it's been trying to teach us. It's when our wounds become our wisdom, our pain becomes our prayer, and our healing becomes our ministry.

If you have ever questioned your faith, your identity, or your belonging—this book is for you. If you've ever wondered how to reconcile who you are with who you were told to be—this book is for you. And if you've ever felt too broken, too different, or too weary to keep believing—know that you are not alone. I have stood in that place. I have wrestled with God there. And I have discovered that even there—especially there—Love does not let go.

My hope is that as you read, you will find pieces of your own story. That you will see your tears in mine, your questions mirrored in my search, and your becoming reflected in the light that keeps breaking through the cracks. You don't have to agree with every idea or share every experience. Just bring your whole self—the honest, curious, weary, wondering self—and let the pages speak to your spirit in their own way.

This is not a book about perfection; it is about process. About learning to hold all that we are with tenderness and truth. About remembering that our scars are not evidence of God's absence but proof of God's presence. Healing doesn't erase what happened, it redeems it.

Because the God who holds the world together is the same God who holds us—fragmented, flawed, and forever becoming whole.

PART I

The Becoming: My Story

1

Girl Meets World

"So God created humankind in his image . . . God blessed them."
— Genesis 1:27–28 (NRSV)

My name is Deiadra Eleece Edwards. I am the middle child of three children born to Gerald and Joan Edwards. I entered this world on February 9, 1973, in Los Angeles, California—fighting for my life. I was born with a hole in my heart and rushed to a children's hospital before my mother ever held me. Death tried to claim me at the very beginning, but it never had power over my purpose. From my first breath, something greater was already speaking for me—something ancient, sacred, and determined. I was marked for life, not by chance, but by calling. Even in the struggle to exist, purpose stood guard over my becoming.

I often tease my mother and say I must have been born under a pew, because as far back as I can remember, church was my second home. It felt like we lived there. The best part of Sundays was always the fried chicken after service—and, of course, the music.

My father is a gifted musician who could play nearly anything his hands touched: piano, organ, trombone, saxophone, guitar, even violin. My father is also a preacher who can either sing the church happy—meaning he can stir the congregation into a joyful, Spirit-filled praise through song—or preach them into heaven. When my brothers and I were old enough to talk, we were old enough to sing. They called us the "Three D's"—Detrick, Deiadra, and Damond. At ages 9, 7, and 6, we were already harmonizing in three parts. Music wasn't just something we did—it was woven into our lives. My parents sang in the adult choir, and we sang with the sunshine band.

Life outside church, though, was not always easy. We struggled financially, and my parents' constant moves between Sacramento—where my mother's family lived—and Los Angeles—where my father's family lived—made life feel unsettled. Still, my parents worked hard to provide, and even those road trips were turned into adventures. Yet beneath the smiles lived a quiet strain—the emotional weariness that comes from trying to make ends meet while holding a family together. I didn't understand it then, but I carried it in my spirit, learning early that love and struggle can ride in the same car.

Then, when I was six years old, came the moment that nearly ended my life. We were in Sacramento, visiting my aunt. One of her sons had been left mentally disabled at birth and struggled with severe seizures, controlled by strong medication. For reasons I still struggle to explain, I decided to take some of his pills. One was Dilantin, which goes directly from the bloodstream to the brain to stop seizures. I don't remember how many I swallowed, but I remember the effects—wobbling when I tried to walk, feeling dizzy and heavy, slipping toward unconsciousness.

My mother and aunt had only gone to the store, leaving us with my cousin Chuckie, who was about 10 years older than me. When they returned, they found me barely responsive. My mom tried to get me to vomit, but it didn't work. They rushed me to the hospital, my head on my mother's lap. The last thing I remember was passing out in her arms.

Later, I learned that I flatlined twice in the emergency room. The doctor told my mother, *"If she lives through the night, she will be a vegetable for the rest of her life."*

I was in a coma for seven days. When I finally woke, it was like being born again. I had to relearn how to walk, talk, and feed myself.

That moment changed me forever. My aunt once said that after that week in the hospital, something in me was different—like part of me had crossed over and returned changed. And in truth, she was right. I was never the same again.

Looking back now, I understand it in both theological and indigenous terms. In the language of my faith, God's hand preserved me. As John 1:5 says, "The light shines in the darkness, and the darkness has not overcome it." In the language of Indigenous wisdom, I had touched the threshold between life and death and returned marked by it. In many traditions—from African cosmology to Native American spirituality—such an experience is seen as an initiation, a calling into deeper awareness of Spirit, energy, and the unseen realms.

From that point on, I carried within me an unshakable truth: death might brush against me, but it could not define me. My life was not an accident. It was an assignment. And even as a child, though I could not name it, my spirit knew—I had been spared for something greater.

From my earliest days, survival became my introduction to the world, and identity became the question I carried within it. Everyone saw me as "the daughter," the only girl, the one who would fulfill the roles and dreams attached to that title. But deep down, even as I learned to smile for pictures and wear the outfits picked for me, I felt a quiet resistance—an unnamed truth that didn't match the story others told about me.

I never liked being a girl. The ruffled socks, the beads and barrettes, the frilly dresses—they just didn't feel like me. At six years old, I may not have had a fully formed sense of self, but I knew I didn't like how I felt when I was all dolled up. My mother, on the other hand, loved it. I was her only daughter, and she took great joy in seeing me dressed in pretty outfits—especially since many of them came from her friends who had no daughters of their own. I was, in a way, the community's little girl.

My cousin Courtney was different. She was allowed to wear jeans, T-shirts, and sweats—the "cool" clothes. Whenever family members bought us outfits, she received the relaxed styles while I was given the dresses. I envied her freedom. Courtney was the youngest of three children born to my mother's sister, my Aunt Gwen—the woman who helped raise me. Although my mother had other siblings, she and Aunt Gwen were the only two daughters in a family of six, and together they raised us as one extended household.

The difference between them was striking. My mother was "saved," shaping our lives with the strict rhythms of church: no pants at church, no dancing, no "worldly" music, and certainly no deviation from the roles assigned to us as "good Christian children." My aunt, though raised the same way, had veered away from those constraints. She raised her children with more freedom, less restriction, and far less dogma.

That freedom showed in Courtney's life. She wore trendy clothes, listened to R&B on the radio, and danced without fear of judgment. Those things weren't just activities—they were symbols. For me, they symbolized choice, expression, and joy. I didn't mind missing the music or the dancing, but the clothes were harder to ignore. Clothing carried weight in my world. It told you who you were supposed to be before you even opened your mouth.

When Courtney put on her jeans and sneakers, it was like her clothes declared "freedom." When I put on a dress, mine declared "expectation." Even as a child, I knew the difference. It was more than fabric—it was theology stitched into our identities. Every outfit was a silent sermon about worth, belonging, and who we were allowed to be. The theology that shaped me taught that holiness could be hemmed, that righteousness could be measured by the modesty of a skirt or the crispness of a collar. What we wore wasn't just about appearance—it was about acceptance.

From an Indigenous and spiritual perspective, I can now see that clothing was never just about covering the body—it was about carrying an identity, an energy. Across cultures, garments have always carried meaning: the warrior's attire signaling readiness for battle, the priest's robes marking them as mediators of the sacred, the dancer's regalia embodying rhythm and story. What we wear has always been more than fashion—it is a language of the soul.

As a child, I already understood this truth, even if I could not articulate it. My cousin's clothes spoke of freedom—bright, expressive, alive. Mine spoke of captivity—carefully chosen to keep me safe within the boundaries of what faith and family deemed "right." And somewhere between the two, I began to sense that God was larger than the rules we'd sewn into our seams.

By this time in my life, we had moved to Sacramento for good. My dad was working as a school bus driver for the local district, and we lived in a three-bedroom apartment where I shared a room with my younger brother. It was in that small, crowded space that I began to feel disconnected from the little girl I was expected to be. My brothers had each other, bound by "boy games" that I was not invited into. I was left alone, surrounded by dolls I didn't want to play with, wishing I could trade places—wishing I was a boy.

I didn't have the language to explain my discomfort. The wider world in the early 1980s was celebrating women's expanding rights—women were running for office, breaking into male-dominated fields, and challenging workplace harassment. But in my smaller world, a girl's worth was still measured by her ability to be a good wife, a good mother, and a good homemaker. My life had been outlined before I could dream it for myself.

Looking back, I realize I was already sensing what theologians and indigenous elders alike affirm: that destiny cannot be scripted by human categories. Spirit resists confinement. Just as rivers carve their own paths regardless of the boundaries drawn on a map, my identity was pressing against the limits of "girlhood" that others had assigned me. The dolls on my shelf were not toys to me—they were silent reminders of an identity I could not inhabit. And every time I wished I was a boy, I wasn't longing to become someone else—I was reaching for the freedom to become who I already was.

I was raised in a strict Christian home, where God's creation of "male and female" in Genesis 1:27 was taught as a fixed binary. My role as "female" was divinely assigned—no pants in church, no sports with the boys, no imagining a future outside marriage to a man. Looking back now, I see the theological weight of that message. Genesis 1 says more than "male and female." It says humankind was made in God's image, blessed equally, and given the same commission: "Be fruitful . . . and have dominion." There was no hierarchy in Eden, no instruction that one image-bearer must rule over the other.

My early discomfort wasn't mere stubbornness—it was an instinct that something about our interpretation of God's intent for humanity was incomplete. Eventually, my mom loosened the rules. I could wear pants. I played softball in summer camp. I even saw women in church who worked construction, drove trucks, and labored in what we called "men's jobs." For a moment, I thought: *Great—I can do what I want as a girl.* But puberty had other plans.

Breasts. A menstrual cycle. My body was becoming what the world called "woman," whether I wanted it to or not. I thought avoiding girly clothes and activities would keep me from being a girl, but biology was indifferent to my resistance. I didn't have the language of "gender identity" back then, but I knew this much: if we are made in the image of God, then our deepest truths must be rooted in spirit, not just in body.

The changing shape of my body forced me to confront the life I was expected to live—boyfriend, marriage, sex, children. I always wanted to be a parent, but the thought of pregnancy repulsed me. Sex with a man held no appeal, and I couldn't imagine carrying a baby inside me.

Marriage and family weren't abstract topics for me; they were loaded with the weight of my own family's story. My parents divorced when I was 10. I still remember my mother asking us who we wanted to live with. My brothers chose to stay with my dad, but I wanted to stay with my mom—partly out of loyalty, partly because I thought she needed me, and partly because, as a girl, I needed her to show me how to be. I wanted to know what love looked like through her eyes, what strength sounded like in her voice. It hurt me to feel as though she would have preferred that I stay with my dad. That feeling came not from her words, but from her absence, from the distance I sensed between what I needed and what she could give.

In time, my dad moved out, and we all ended up staying with my mom. But her absence at home soon became as real as my father's physical absence. She seemed to spend more time away from us, and the space between us widened until our relationship felt distant—almost unfamiliar. She poured her energy into other people, leaving me to navigate my loneliness. My dad would remarry and that would cause even more challenges in our lives.

During my junior high years, life shifted suddenly. My mom fell ill and went to stay with my aunt. In her absence, my dad returned to care for us, filling the house with a presence that felt both familiar and strange. Familiar, because I had missed his voice, his laughter, the way his energy filled a room. Strange, because so much had changed since he left—the rhythms of our lives, the quiet tension that settled between my parents, and the way I had learned to guard parts of myself. His return brought both comfort and confusion, a reminder of what once was and of all that could never be again. For two years, it felt golden—family nights filled with laughter, movies, and a sense of wholeness I had longed for. Then, just as suddenly, it ended. One weekend, he packed up and left for good.

Later, my mom sat me down and said, "*I gave him a choice—his woman or his kids. He chose his woman.*" My heart shattered. Back in my bedroom, I found his stereo sitting on the floor and a handwritten note: *Daddy loves you always.*

In that moment, love felt like abandonment, and I made a vow I thought I'd never break: I would never forgive him.

From then on, every man was my father. I measured them against the pain of his absence. And in my mind, having children meant risking the same mistakes my parents made. But something else was stirring in me—something I didn't yet have words for.

I was attracted to girls. I didn't understand it fully, but it felt natural, even comforting. I dated boys to fit in, offering them what they wanted physically as long as they didn't ask for more. But these "relationships" only confirmed what I already sensed: I wasn't meant to be in love with a man.

Loneliness pressed in and so did depression. My brothers had each other, my friends dated, and I felt invisible. The world I was born into felt cruel, but somewhere in me, there was a whisper of another world—one I would someday create for myself.

Over time, I learned the truth about my father's leaving—he hadn't abandoned me out of indifference, and he never spoke ill of my mother.

That shifted something in me. I wanted to be like him in the ways he had been good: protective, attentive, honoring. I imagined myself as the one buying flowers, opening doors, carrying the bags—the one providing. It all made sense to me.

But the world I lived in told me, *No, Deiadra, you can't think like that. It will never happen.* So I tucked that dream away like a fairytale I might never have the courage to open.

Yet even then, I now see, the image of God in me was pressing against the boundaries, urging me toward the truth: *This is not all there is. Keep looking. Keep becoming.*

2

Girl Meets Boy

"It is not good for the human to be alone; I will make a helper as his counterpart."

— Genesis 2:18 (NRSV)

By the time I reached my late teens, I had learned to perform the role that the world expected of me. I could dress the part, smile when appropriate, and even convince others that I was comfortable in my own skin. But beneath that polished surface, I was restlessly searching for the elusive bridge between who I knew myself to be and who everyone else insisted I was.

Depression became my closest companion. I carried it everywhere like an invisible shadow, pressing in at every quiet moment. There were nights when I didn't want to die, but I no longer wanted to keep living this way. I often felt like I wanted to die—though somewhere deep within, I knew what I truly desired was life. I just couldn't see how to reach it. Hope felt too far away, too heavy to hold. Yet even in my numbness, a small, stubborn spark refused to go out—a quiet knowing that life still had something sacred left for me. And still, Sunday after Sunday, church offered a kind of reprieve—not freedom, not healing, at least not yet, but an escape. Directing the choir gave me purpose. Music gave me permission to smile. And for a few fleeting moments, when the voices rose and the harmonies swelled, I could breathe again.

It was during that season that I met Shawn. Our introduction was ordinary, the kind of moment you might miss if you weren't paying attention. But his presence left a mark. He looked at me with a kind of curiosity that unsettled me, as if he could see past the carefully constructed mask and glimpse something truer—something I wasn't ready to name. That gaze was exhilarating and terrifying all at once. It was the first time I felt both exposed and seen, as though the very thing I'd tried to hide was quietly asking to be acknowledged.

We started talking, then spent more time together. Before long, a connection formed that neither of us could deny. For the first time, I felt seen—not just for what I could do or the role I played, but for who I was in moments of stillness. It felt like discovering a missing piece of myself. Love, or at least what I understood love to be then, wrapped itself around me like a warm blanket.

But love is rarely simple.

In private, I let my guard down. I could drop the mask, laugh freely, and speak from places that didn't fit neatly into the labels of "woman" or "girlfriend." In public, though, we slipped into roles scripted by tradition and expectation. He was the strong protector; I, the nurturing companion. We weren't simply in a relationship, we were staging one, performing for the approval of others.

That performance began to exhaust me. The more I tried to conform, the more distance I felt between who I was and who I was pretending to be. At times, I wondered if my attraction to him was less about who he was and more about what he represented—a longing for freedom, for someone to truly see me, even the parts I couldn't yet name. The relationship ended when he returned to his ex, who eventually became his wife. I told myself it was a sign—that I wasn't meant to be with men, that love had its own language, one I still didn't know how to speak. What I couldn't see then was how deeply I'd equated rejection with unworthiness, how easily I mistook silence for fate. It wasn't that I was unlovable—it was that I hadn't yet learned to love myself without apology.

In time, that quiet longing for acceptance began to turn inward, shaping how I saw myself and the world around me.

Sometime later, while visiting my mother at work in Montgomery Ward, I wandered into the men's department. Rows of tailored suits, pressed shirts, and polished shoes called to me. I matched shirts with ties, imagined textures against fabrics, and arranged color palettes in my mind. For a brief, electric moment, I saw myself in those clothes—saw the reflection of the person I longed to become.

When my mother asked where I'd been, I told a small lie: "Just in the men's department, imagining what it would be like to buy suits for my husband." Inside, though, I whispered, *Lord, forgive me,* because the truth was different. I wasn't imagining a husband. I was imagining myself. But that truth was too heavy to speak aloud, so I carried it in silence, and the silence deepened my depression.

It was around this time that I met a young woman from a nearby church. We became close friends, and eventually I moved in with her to help care for her son. At first, I believed it was simply friendship. But companionship shifted into attraction, and for the first time, I experienced intimacy that felt real, alive, undeniable. It was both thrilling and terrifying, because it awakened parts of me I had been taught to deny.

From the perspective of the church, this was sin. I had grown up believing same-sex attraction was outside God's will, and I carried that teaching like a chain. My heart pulled me one way, but my theology pulled me another. I didn't yet know that the theology I inherited was incomplete—that it had been shaped more by human fear than divine truth.

I remember wrestling late into the night with the scriptures I had been taught. The Genesis story was always used to defend "one man, one woman." But as I studied more deeply, I noticed something that had been overlooked: "It is not good for the human to be alone" (Gen. 2:18). God's solution was relationship, not a rigid formula. The text never insisted that companionship must only take one form to be blessed.

Looking back, I see that the joy I felt with her—the laughter, the comfort, the deep sense of being known—was not contrary to God's will. It bore the fruit scripture names as the evidence of God's Spirit: love, joy, peace, kindness, gentleness, faithfulness (Gal. 5:22–23). The problem wasn't that God had rejected me. The problem was that my theology had no room for me.

Though that relationship ended, my longing for authenticity remained. I buried it under ministry, convincing myself that if I worked hard enough, preached passionately enough, sang earnestly enough, the "wrong" parts of me would disappear. But God has a way of refusing to be boxed in. Slowly, I began to sense that the One who formed me had no interest in erasing the parts of me that felt most alive.

Genesis says we are created in God's image. If that is true, then God's image must include the complexity of human identity—including mine. My attraction to women wasn't evidence of my failure; it was evidence that God's image was far broader than human tradition had allowed.

As I entered my twenties, that search for authenticity only intensified. I found myself drawn into a complicated relationship with an older woman from my church—a woman I came to call my "god mom." What began as a nurturing bond became something more, stretching across a decade of secrecy and longing. By all accounts, it should have driven me further from God, but in that space, I also discovered the contours of my own masculinity. With her, I wasn't content to play the role of "woman." I wanted to be the man in the relationship, though I rarely spoke it aloud.

At twenty-five, I enlisted in the military, hoping to find courage and clarity. For the first time, away from family and church judgment, I allowed myself to live openly, even briefly, as the person I had long known inside. It was liberating. I promised myself I wouldn't go back. But an injury cut my service short, and I returned home, back into the arms of old patterns.

The years that followed were marked by cycles of secrecy, ministry, and attempts at celibacy. I tried to convince myself that discipline could fix desire. I told myself if I prayed enough, God would deliver me. But each time I walked away from love, I felt more fractured.

By the time I turned thirty, I was exhausted. I had tasted love, but only in secret. I had known authenticity, but only in fragments. I longed for a relationship I could live out loud. Preparing to adopt a son, I knew I could no longer pretend. I gave away every piece of women's clothing I owned and filled my closet with jeans, *ribbed tank tops (often called "wife-beaters")*, and suits. I will never forget the first suit I bought—hat and all. Sliding it on, I felt something break open inside me. It wasn't just clothing. It was liberation. It was the weight of falsehoods lifting, the birth of a self I had always known but never given permission to exist. That day, I met him—the boy, the man, the truth of me. He was here to stay.

And when I look back to that moment in Montgomery Ward, standing among the suits, I now recognize it as holy. God was there, even if I didn't yet have the words. That quiet recognition of myself—hidden in plain sight—was the Spirit's whisper: *You are still Mine. You are still in My image. And one day, you will live it out loud.*

3

The Search for Me

"For You created my inmost being; You knit me together in my mother's womb. I praise You because I am fearfully and wonderfully made."

— Psalm 139:13–14(NRSV)

I have spent most of my life searching.

In the beginning, it was love—a mother's love, a father's love. As a child of divorced parents, I silently carried the weight of my father's absence, wondering if it was somehow my fault. My mother never said it was, but her distance after the divorce spoke louder than words.

She found comfort in other people and their children—buying them clothes, taking them places, laughing with them. She did all the things I longed for her to do with me. I would hear her laughter in another room, not for me but for someone else's child, and I learned early that joy was something I could hear but not always hold.

My brothers had each other. I had my questions:

Why wasn't I enough?

What was wrong with me?

I longed for her nurture, her tenderness, for her to hold me and say, "*It's not your fault.* That day never came.

Over the years, I was blessed to have strong women take me under their wings—women who asked about my feelings, hugged me, and told me they loved me. They embraced the broken little girl inside, but no matter how much they gave, the emptiness remained.

As I grew older, my search shifted. I stopped looking for my mother's love and started looking for romantic love. Maybe, I thought, if I got married and raised a family, the void would finally go away.

I was engaged three times—each time to a man—and each time I walked away.

The first was at eighteen, fresh out of high school, to a man twenty years my senior, an ordained elder raising three children alone. He was kind enough, but I wasn't in love with him, and I couldn't imagine stepping into motherhood that young.

The second was to a young man from Oregon, part of a church our congregation fellowshipped with annually. We met, exchanged calls, and I convinced myself I could grow to love him. But even with the ring on my finger, I knew I was lying to us both. I ended it before I could walk into a marriage built on pretending. The last engagement wasn't about love at all—it was about not being alone. I was already involved with a married woman at the time (a story for another chapter), and he seemed safe: funny, patient, and not pressuring me into sex. But when I learned he had spoken about me disrespectfully to my uncle, I ended it on the spot, dropping the rings at his job without a second thought.

By then, I could no longer deny the truth: I wasn't drawn to men at all. It was women who stirred my heart. Saying it out loud was like releasing a weight I had carried for years. I told myself, *maybe a woman can bring me the happiness I deserve.* But even in relationships with women, something was still missing. I was looking for love to save me, to fill the holes in my soul.

When I took in my son Lawrence at the age of thirty, I thought perhaps parenthood would be the answer. I had always wanted children—though never to give birth myself—but his arrival wasn't planned.

I first met him at church. He was a chubby-cheeked baby with big brown eyes who reached for me one Sunday morning, arms outstretched. I picked him up, and in that instant, something shifted. We bonded quickly. For weeks, his foster caregiver brought him to church, and he would sit with me for the entire service. Then one Sunday, he wasn't there, and my heart sank.

A few weeks later, he returned—this time with someone connected to his foster family who wasn't planning to adopt him. I began the process of getting licensed as a foster parent, and before long, he was in my home. From the moment he was placed in my arms, I felt a love that was unconditional, unafraid, and pure. It didn't measure me against expectations or demand I change to fit a mold. It simply asked that I be present.

Lawrence was the life jacket I didn't know I needed. He gave me a reason to live when depression pressed in. But parenting didn't erase my struggles. I was still missing something, and I began to realize that the love I was searching for wasn't going to come from a partner—or even from my child.

It had to come from me.

I had been expecting others to love me in a way that matched my deepest needs, without realizing that people can only love from the capacity they have. Expecting them to love me exactly as I needed was like asking them to become me. And when I looked honestly at my relationships, I saw a pattern: I had been with people who were already connected to someone else, people who wanted what I could give without being able—or willing—to give in return.

That wasn't love. And the truth was, I didn't love myself either. Admitting the truth was painful, but it shifted everything. For the first time, I turned from an external search for validation to an internal journey of discovery. Psalm 139 declares that I am "fearfully and wonderfully made," yet I had spent years living as though I was unworthy of love, peace, or even my own life.

At thirty-six, standing on the edge of an emotional breakdown, I finally chose a different path. I checked myself into a psychiatric treatment program, determined to confront the trauma of my childhood and begin the work of healing. It was there that I learned to face and manage both depression and attention deficit disorder.

That season became a turning point. I began to put myself first—not in selfishness, but in sacred respect. I learned to honor my life enough to avoid relationships that starved my soul, to refuse to let anyone take me away from myself, and to commit—fully and unapologetically—to my own healing.

I hadn't yet mastered the art of loving myself, but I was learning—and the way forward was finally clear. I was no longer chasing love as a rescuer. I was learning to be whole in myself, to see that everything I needed had been with me all along.

The search wasn't over. But for the first time, it felt attainable. And this time, it wasn't about finding someone to complete me, it was about walking fully in the truth that I was already complete.

When I began to love myself, I could finally see what God had seen all along: I wasn't broken. I was becoming. God's image in me was never something I had to earn—it was the truth that had been there from the beginning.

From a theological and metaphysical perspective, I came to understand that self-love is holy work. It is not selfishness; it is alignment with the Divine. In the wisdom of *Ma'at—the ancient Egyptian principle of truth, balance, and divine order—it is balance restored.* In the voice of the psalmist, it is the recognition that I am "wonderfully made." And in the whispers of my ancestors, it is the healing of wounds carried across generations. To love myself was to love the God within me, and to honor the sacred truth that wholeness is not something I had to find—it was something I had to remember.

4

A Good Life or My Best Life?

The Emergence of AmunDayo Khepra Oloririi

"I came that they may have life, and have it abundantly."
— John 10:10(NRSV)

The spring of 2012 was a turning point—the season I met a part of myself I hadn't known was waiting to be found.

By then, I was in a committed relationship with an amazing woman. We lived in a comfortable home, were raising my son together, and I was stepping into a new career. Life had its challenges, and I still wasn't fully living my truth, but on the surface, life was good—the kind of good that looks whole from the outside but feels incomplete on the inside. It was steady, safe, and respectable, yet something in me remained unsettled. I had built a life that made sense to everyone but me.

One afternoon, my partner told me she'd scheduled an appointment with a Neter Risha High Priestess in Oakland. She had always carried a certain magic about her—a deep connection to indigenous spirituality—and now she was ready to take the next step. I offered to drive, thinking that would be the extent of my involvement. I didn't know I was driving towards my own destiny.

At the High Priestess's home, the air felt different—charged, alive. I felt unexpectedly at home, and that unsettled me. It was a familiarity that bypassed the mind and spoke straight to the spirit.

This was confusing. I had been taught that anything outside "God the Father, God the Son, and God the Holy Spirit" was dangerous, even demonic. Yet surrounded by symbols and rituals I didn't understand, I felt a resonance I couldn't deny.

The woman—who we lovingly call Queen Mother—looked at me with knowing eyes. She invited me to sit, took a sip of rum, spat it at my feet, and said, "The Divine has been waiting for you."

Her words cracked something open. The rest of the moment blurred, but I knew I had been seen in a way that defied explanation. I didn't yet know what God wanted with me, but a seed was planted. As I followed the path of initiation, I began to learn what it meant to walk in the Neter Risha tradition.

It wasn't merely ritual or ceremony. It was remembering what had always been true:

The Divine is in all things. God is not confined to pews or pulpits. The same Spirit I felt in church is present in the rhythm of the drum, the whisper of trees, the flow of water, and the breath that sustains me. God had never abandoned me; God was everywhere I turned.

Balance is life. In the language of Ma'at, wholeness comes from harmony. I was wrestling with imbalance—between who I presented to the world and who I knew myself to be. The walk of priesthood invited me to stop choosing halves and embrace my whole self.

The ancestors walk with us. Those who came before us are not gone; they live in memory, bone, and prayer. I realized I was not carrying my journey alone. Their strength ran through me, whispering, *keep going—your destiny is tied to ours.*

Priesthood is service. A priest is not a status but a responsibility: a vessel for healing, a bridge between seen and unseen, a servant to community. It meant no longer shrinking from my story.

What I survived was not just for me—it was for those who would need my testimony.

Truth is freedom. Masks are heavy; authenticity sets the spirit free. I had been living a "good" life, not my "best" life. Freedom wasn't in denial but in embracing truth, even when it cost me something.

These were not abstractions. They spoke directly to my contradictions—holding tradition while feeling Spirit's pull to expand, presenting as one thing while knowing I was another, loving God while questioning the theology I had inherited. Neter Risha gave me language for what I had always felt but could not name. I wasn't broken. I was becoming.

That day marked the beginning of my initiation as a priest-in-training. For one year, I wore white as a sign of commitment. I studied the history of the African diaspora and learned that God's presence is revealed not only in church pews but also in the wind through trees, the movement of water, the cadence of song, and the energy connecting all living things. My understanding of God expanded—beyond the boxes I'd inherited—toward a Creator far more vast, intimate, and inclusive than I had ever been taught.

When I completed my initiation, I was given the name *AmunDayo Khepra Olooririi—son who has a great head, has grand destiny, and self-made joy.*

"Son?" The word startled me. I still saw myself as a dual spirit—a masculine-presenting female. I connected the name not to gender but to spirit. I believed I had arrived at authenticity and freedom.

By the end of 2012, my partner and I formalized our relationship as domestic partners. We had been living together since 2010, but this step marked something deeper—a sense of stability and shared purpose. Our home was filled with love, our family was growing stronger, and our lives felt steady. I thought I had reached the mountaintop.

Then came January 1, 2014.

It was New Year's morning. We had attended a Watch Night Service, ringing in the year with worship, prayer, and gratitude. We were still in bed, talking about our hopes, when my phone rang.

It was my regional bishop. Her voice was heavy. "Bobbie Jean is gone," she said.

The name hit me like a stone.

Bobbie Jean Baker wasn't just a friend. She was my sister, my mentor, an unapologetic woman of trans experience, a powerful Black trans leader who survived HIV, addiction, and the streets and turned survival into ministry: advocacy, community care, and fierce love. She spoke into my life with clarity that left no room for hiding and loved me in a way that made pretense impossible.

She could cut through my defenses with one sentence. Tilting her head with that sideways smile, she'd say, "Baby, you're all boy." Not accusation but affirmation—naming what she saw long before I had the courage to see it. I laughed it off, insisting I was fine as a masculine-presenting lesbian. She never argued. She let the truth rest between us like a seed, waiting for its season.

After her death, that seed refused to stay buried. I heard her voice in my spirit: *When are you going to transition?* It wasn't loud, but it was persistent. Weeks later, in prayer, another voice—unmistakably God's—rose within me: *Do you want to live a good life or your best life?*

I froze. I had a good life—a wife I loved, a son I adored, a growing ministry, work I enjoyed. But "good" suddenly felt like a safe compromise. My best life—the abundant life Jesus speaks of in John 10:10—would cost more. It would require stepping fully into the truth Bobbie Jean had seen in me.

When I told my wife I wanted to transition, the conversation was raw. She was honest: she had never wanted to be with a trans man. If she could not stay in the marriage, she would leave. I told her I understood, but I could no longer deny who God created me to be. Jesus says, "Whoever wants to save their life will lose it, but whoever loses their life for me will save it" (Luke 9:24). For me, losing my life meant letting go of others' images of me—even if it meant losing relationships I cherished. What I stood to gain—my whole, authentic self—was worth it.

By April 2014, I had begun therapy as part of the medical transition process, meeting regularly with my endocrinologist to prepare for hormone therapy. On the morning of May 6, I stood before my altar, took a deep breath, and prayed: *Lord, make me an exception.* Then I went to Kaiser and received my first testosterone injection. From that day forward, God has honored that prayer.

By "exception," I didn't mean better than anyone. I meant free from the limiting narratives society places on trans men—the misconceptions, the pressure to overcompensate with hyper-masculinity, the demand to live completely "stealth" just to survive. I didn't want secrecy or stereotypes. My prayer was a declaration: that my journey would be defined by authenticity, balance, and divine purpose—a testament to God's calling that could reshape not only how the world sees us, but how we see ourselves.

In November 2014, it became official—on my birth certificate, Social Security card, and driver's license. *Deiadra* had lovingly stepped aside to allow *AmunDayo* to emerge. She is not gone. She lives with me. I honor her for holding things together for forty years. Even when we wanted to give up, she pressed forward. We are integrated now, and she remains the best part of me.

My journey mirrors a pattern in scripture. Abram became Abraham. Sarai became Sarah. Simon became Peter. Saul became Paul. Each name change marked not only a new season of purpose but a divine affirmation of identity—not the creation of a new person from nothing, but the revelation of who they had been all along. My emergence as *AmunDayo Khepra Oloririi* is the same. Deiadra was the steward of my survival; AmunDayo is the steward of my flourishing. Together, we carry the testimony of 2 Corinthians 5:17: "If anyone is in Christ, the new creation has come: The old has gone, the new is here!"

But as I stepped fully into myself, my family was asked to walk their own transformation. My transition pulled everyone connected to me into their own wrestling with identity, love, and faith.

I will never forget a conversation with my mother. Our relationship had grown closer than ever. As I drove her to an appointment, she asked quietly, "Are you thinking about transitioning?" At that point, I hadn't decided. "I haven't really thought about it," I said.

She paused, then asked, "Why does God love you more?"

Startled, I asked, "What do you mean?"

"Because God gave you the opportunity to choose."

She meant God loved me enough to allow me the freedom to choose who I would be. She didn't know it then, but she was prophetic. That sentence reframed everything. I realized I wasn't merely offered a choice—I was *called* to choose. And I did. To my surprise, my mother handled my transition with far more grace than my coming out as same-gender-loving. Her love expanded to meet me where I was.

My father was different. Distance made avoidance easy; he lived in St. Louis. When I identified as a lesbian, nothing seemed to change for him—I was still his baby girl. Transition felt like another matter altogether. When I finally gathered the courage to tell him, I discovered he already knew—and had accepted it. At the time, he was incarcerated—wrongly convicted through a manipulated plea deal. Prison forced him into stillness, and in that stillness he read: books, stories, articles, testimonies about the trans experience. His consciousness shifted. When I told him, he didn't hesitate. I was his son without question. That affirmation steadied my world.

My brothers had their own paths. My younger brother, Damond, struggled with my sexuality at first but grew to accept me. My transition flowed more easily for him. Detrick, my oldest brother, carried a protector's mantle and held to traditional Christian beliefs. For years he insisted I would never be his brother.

Other relatives wrestled too—especially my Uncle Teddy. But there were champions: my Aunt Gwen, who loved me without condition, and my cousin Courtney, who once said she believed I had made a "quantum leap," like the old TV show—that when I flatlined at six years old and came back, I returned not as the girl I had been but as the boy I was meant to be. For me, it sounded like revelation.

Over time, my family grew more comfortable, though pronouns and my name were stumbling blocks. My wife was hurt that I rarely corrected them. She read it as fear or weakness. The truth was, they had known Deiadra for forty years. I couldn't expect overnight change. They had their own transition to walk, and I loved them enough to give them grace.

I didn't realize then that my wife also needed that same grace. She, too, was transitioning—learning how to see, love, and live with the man I was becoming. I wish I had given her more space in the beginning. By the mercy of the Divine, I learned that love means not only asking for grace but extending it.

Now our family is whole. Detrick calls me his brother. Uncle Teddy embraces the man I am. My family strives to use the right pronouns and my chosen name. Their acceptance was a sacred journey. We were all in transition together.

Through a theological lens, their struggle reminds me of Jacob wrestling with God through the night (Genesis 32). Jacob would not let go without a blessing, and he walked away with a limp—a reminder that transformation is not painless. My family wrestled with God's revelation in me—their theology, memories, traditions, and fears—and did not come away unchanged.

It was also their wilderness. As Israel wandered forty years learning to see themselves as God's people, my family needed time to release the familiar image of "Deiadra" and embrace the reality of AmunDayo. They, too, crossed a Red Sea, wandered through confusion, and arrived at a promised land of acceptance.

Metaphysically, transition is not an individual act but a communal initiation. When one person shifts, everyone connected to them is invited to shift. Their resistance, stumbles, and eventual embrace were part of the Divine choreography—an invitation to expand their understanding of love, identity, and God.

From an indigenous perspective, it was ancestral healing. Families carry wounds of silence and rejection. Walking through my transition together repaired threads in our lineage. We taught future generations that love can evolve, acceptance can be learned, and the Divine shows up even in our wrestling.

Their struggle was not failure; it was formation. Today, when I hear my brother say "brother," or my father say "son," those words carry the weight of a hard-won blessing—like Jacob's limp, like Israel's promised land, like an ancestor's whisper finally reaching home.

This is what it means to follow Christ into abundant life—not simply the promise of heaven after death, but the courage to live fully here and now as the person God imagined before you were formed in your mother's womb. And as if to seal that revelation with purpose, that same October the Divine called me to birth something larger than myself: the *Integrated Praise Spiritual Center (IPSC).*

Launching a ministry in the midst of my own transition felt almost impossible. I questioned whether I was worthy or ready, and whether people would follow a pastor daring to live outside traditional boxes. Yet God's timing was undeniable. On October 4, 2014, IPSC was born—not with polished institutional clarity, but with a trembling "yes." Over time, that "yes" blossomed into a vision: *Loving People to Healing—fostering life, unity, and freedom through spiritual integration.*

Theologically, IPSC embodies *incarnation*—God becoming visible in and through people. Metaphysically, it proclaims that wholeness comes through integration—we refuse to live in fragments. The church mirrored my own journey: as I wove together Deiadra and AmunDayo, IPSC was called to weave together faith and freedom, scripture and Spirit, prayer and praxis.

From an indigenous lens, IPSC carries *sankofa*—going back to fetch what was lost. It honors ancestral wisdom that knows healing flows through song, dance, drum, circle, and community care. IPSC is not only about doctrine but remembering: the Divine dwells in the circle of community, in the rhythm of breath, in the pulse of the earth.

"Integrated" means refusing to separate what God has joined soul and body, faith and justice, tradition and liberation. "Praise" is more than music; it is a lifestyle of gratitude, resilience, and resistance. "Spiritual Center" means we are more than a church: a sanctuary for seekers, a refuge for the wounded, a training ground for justice, a circle where love, Spirit, and liberation converge.

Looking back, IPSC was not just my ministry, it was my initiation. It was the outward expression of the inward work of integration. My identity and the church's identity are inseparable testimonies: abundant life is found where truth, Spirit, and freedom embrace without apology.

God also blessed my wife and me with an unexpected gift: children—not by biology, but by Spirit. Young people—some barely younger than us, others a generation below—found their way to us seeking guidance, direction, or a safe place to land. Over time, many began to see us as spiritual parents. Some came from broken family ties. Others from loss. Still others because they saw something in us their souls needed.

While many honor the mother-and-father spirit we carry, a core group became the nucleus of our family: *Sara, Peter, Taliyah, Howard, Sajian & Marjah, Leon & Kiki, and Imani & L.A, and of course, Lawrence (now Correen) my beautiful trans daughter.* Alongside them is *Malcolm*, my wife's adopted son, who was already part of her journey before I arrived, and 7 amazing grandchildren. Most of the children are near our age, which may seem unusual, but chronology never diminished the bond. Connection did the binding. Each brought love, laughter, challenge, and perspective. They carried us as much as we carried them.

Some days I feel unworthy of such a gift, but I honor it as one of my life's greatest blessings: the call to fatherhood. To be trusted with the hearts of people, especially those who've endured loss, rejection, or displacement—is sacred. In them, I see God's promise that family is not limited to bloodline but flows wherever love, commitment, and Spirit create belonging.

I often think of Jesus stretching out his hand toward his disciples: "Here are my mother and my brothers . . . whoever does the will of my Father in heaven is my brother and sister and mother"

(Matthew 12:49–50). Family is more than biology; it is divine connection, forged in purpose and sealed in love.

Metaphysically, fatherhood is impartation—energy, guidance, presence. It is being an anchor for those whose lives have been fractured. From an indigenous perspective, chosen family heals ancestral lines, restoring what was broken by creating belonging in the present.

Our children remind me daily that fatherhood is not perfection but presence—not having all the answers but walking alongside as they find their own. They have brought more life and love than we imagined. In them, I see another expression of God's promise: a family born not only of blood, but of Spirit. This is my best life, and the greater is still to come.

The abundant life Jesus offers is not the easiest road. It asks for surrender and courage. It asks us—and those who love us—to wrestle, to wander, and to relearn what love means. But it is the road where the spirit finally breathes, where truth stands uncovered, where family learns to see as God sees, where the ancestors nod in agreement, and where purpose meets us in full view.

5

Being Jeremiah

"Before I formed you in the womb I knew you . . . I appointed you."
— *Jeremiah 1:5 (NRSV)*

Jeremiah's story has always gripped me because it is not the tale of a man who sought power or position—it is the testimony of someone who could not escape God's voice, even when it pulled him into places that made him unpopular, uncomfortable, and misunderstood.

A major prophet with a major assignment, Jeremiah was called to speak truth to a fallen nation—truth they did not want to hear. What first struck me about him was his disbelief in his own ability. When God called him, his response was: *"How can I speak? I am only a child."* His fear wasn't just about the weight of the message—it was about how he would be received. In his mind, he was too young, too inexperienced, too small for the task.

But God didn't accept his excuse. God promised to put words in his mouth and courage in his bones. In a dramatic sign of that anointing, God touched Jeremiah's lips with a burning coal. Then came the question: *"What do you see?"*

Jeremiah answered, *"A walking stick."* God replied, *"Good eyes; I'm sticking with you. I will hasten to perform my word."* Scripture doesn't fully describe the object Jeremiah saw, and I've often imagined God was showing him something deeper—that whatever Jeremiah dared to envision, God would move quickly to bring it into being.

That moment has always felt personal to me, because my own call to ministry was tangled in questions about adequacy—not of age, but of identity. Jeremiah's challenge was his youth. Mine was my existence as a trans man in a church culture that had taught me my very being was a sin.

I was in my thirties when I finally said yes to God's call. By then, I had already been privately silenced when I came out, and now God was asking me to stand publicly and declare a radically inclusive message to a community that had been told they were outside of God's love.

Five years earlier, I had been attending a local Church of God in Christ congregation. In many ways, this was home. I was raised in this church, and much of my early ministry had been shaped there. I had gone from being the first teenager to serve as head of the choir to beginning my journey as an *Aspiring Missionary—a woman in training for ministry and service within the COGIC tradition.* I watched that ministry grow and change—not only in leadership but even in its name. It went from Good Samaritan Cathedral II, COGIC to Labour of Love COGIC. By that time, the pastor and First Last, (Pastor's wife) Rev. Rickey & Missionary Madelynn Tates. They weren't just leaders to me; they became my spiritual parents in one of the most fragile seasons of my life.

I loved them deeply. Mom and I were especially close—she was someone I could talk to about anything, even my feelings for women. She never judged me or loved me less. Dad, on the other hand, was the kind of pastor who could love you fiercely and rebuke you just as quickly. I respected him for both.

Still, I struggled with my sexuality in that ministry. During this season, I secretly became involved with an older woman in the church. I never told anyone, but when it ended, I spent years trying to "pray the gay away." No matter how hard I tried, I could not erase who I was. Eventually, I had to be honest—not just with myself, but with my pastor, my dad.

By then, I had just started preaching. I spoken at my local church on Friday nights, as well as at district and state meetings. My ministry was taking off. One Friday evening, Pastor Tates called and asked if I was coming to service, and if I would be willing to preach. Normally, I never missed a service. But when I heard his voice that night, the pressure inside me could no longer be contained.

I told him the truth. I told him I was struggling with my sexuality. I confessed that I no longer saw my desire as sin and that I believed God had called me to live authentically.

His response pierced me: *"Well, I guess that means you're no longer on the praise team or in the choir."* That was it. No acknowledgement of the struggle. No prayer, no space for conversation. We never spoke of it again. And I never returned to that church.

One day, while lying in bed, I felt a breeze against my skin. There was no open window, no fan, no air conditioner running. The sunlight streaming through the glass seemed brighter than usual. Before I could question it, I heard God whisper: *"Before you were born, I knew you."*

Peace washed over me. God was telling me that nothing about me was a surprise. I was known, chosen, called—not in spite of who I was, but because of it. God wasn't asking me to become someone else first. God was asking me to speak from exactly who I was.

Still, I wrestled. How could I walk this out in Sacramento—the city where everyone knew my history? I thought about moving somewhere new, where no one had known me as female. But God made it clear: *Here is where you will walk out this process.*

Then came the question again: *"What do you see?"*

I began to weep. I wasn't sure I dared to answer. Eventually, exhaustion pulled me into sleep, and I dreamed I was in the jungle wrestling with a lion.

At first, terror surged through me. His golden mane flashed like fire, his roar split the sky, and his weight pressed me into the earth. Surely this meant I would be devoured. Every instinct told me to fight, to run, to save myself.

But as the struggle wore on, something shifted. His eyes met mine—not with hunger, but with recognition. His breath was warm against my face, steady, unhurried, as if he had no intention of harming me. His claws, though sharp, did not tear. His strength was undeniable, yet it held me rather than crushed me.

And in that moment I realized: I wasn't fighting for my life. I was resisting his embrace. The lion was not my enemy. He was my mirror. He carried both ferocity and tenderness, wildness and wisdom. He was the Christ I had feared, the ancestor I had forgotten, the masculine spirit within me that I had long refused to name.

What I thought would devour me was actually trying to claim me. The lion was not there to kill me, but to hold me—to fold me into a strength I didn't know I carried. His embrace was not destruction. It was initiation.

Weeks later, one of my spiritual mothers called. She said God told her my name had been changed: I was no longer Jacob but Israel, because I had wrestled with an angel and prevailed. I remembered my dream immediately and went to reread Jacob's story. In a Rembrandt painting of the scene, I noticed the angel wasn't wrestling Jacob—he was holding him. Jacob was the one struggling against the embrace.

I understood. The challenge wasn't fighting God; it was surrendering to being held. It is easier to fight the unknown than to rest in it. Looking back, that lion in my dream was God—powerful, unshakable, holding me when I wanted to run.

And like Jeremiah, my fear wasn't about my ability to speak—it was about daring to believe I could be great in the eyes of the One who sent me.

When God asked again, *"What do you see?"* I finally answered: "I see a world travailing in anguish, longing for peace. I want to create a space where people can find the God of their understanding—no religion, no dogma, just pure love and light."

God's response was the same as to Jeremiah: *"I will hasten to make it so."*

Accepting that call has meant living like Jeremiah—often unpopular, misunderstood, sometimes rejected before I even speak. There have been moments I stood in the pulpit knowing my very presence was a protest against narrow theology. And yet, Jeremiah 20:9 has burned in me: *"His word is in my heart like a fire, a fire shut up in my bones; I am weary of holding it in; indeed, I cannot."*

Over time, I realized the greatness God saw in me was not something to be earned—it was already there. The real work was to believe it. I wrestled through seminary. I wrestled while building my ministry. Slowly, the wrestling gave way to resting—trusting that the same God who called me had already equipped me.

Over ten years later, I am pastoring a ministry rooted in loving people into healing. We teach not religion but relationship—relationship with God, with self, and with each other. Like Jeremiah, I have been called to show people a better way: not just to live a good life, but their best life.

Being Jeremiah for my generation means leaving fear behind, focusing on the present instead of the past, my strengths instead of my weaknesses. God has anointed my mouth—not with coal this time, but with the authority to call forth what I see. And I see a future where God's love cannot be contained by human boundaries—a future where the fire in my bones keeps burning, not for my sake, but to light the way for others who have been told they are outside God's reach.

Accepting my call as a prophet in this generation has meant living at the intersection of my personal truth and God's larger vision for humanity. My journey—from Deiadra to AmunDayo, from hiding to living in the open, from questioning God's choice to embracing it—has not only been about gender or identity. It has been about learning to see the world through God's eyes and refusing to shrink that vision to fit human boundaries.

Although I never returned to my old church except for special occasions, I believe my godparents loved me, and perhaps in their own way were proud that I chose to live true to myself, even if they could not embrace it publicly. Both passed before we had the chance to reconcile, but their spiritual visitations in my dreams remind me of our closeness and their labor of love.

From a metaphysical perspective, I see now that the lion's embrace, Jeremiah's fire, and my godparents' love are all threads of the same truth: Spirit is always calling us to integration. What we resist most fiercely is often the very thing meant to heal us. My wrestling was never about defeating God or escaping my identity—it was about learning to surrender into wholeness.

From an indigenous lens, I recognize that my journey was not mine alone but part of a larger circle. The ancestors were guiding me, even in my dreams, through symbols of strength and balance. The lion, the fire, the whispered breeze—all were messages from beyond reminding me that I walk not only for myself but for those who came before and those who will come after. In our traditions, initiation is never for the individual alone; it is for the healing of the community.

This is what my story has taught me: prophecy is not simply about foretelling the future, but about embodying a truth that sets others free. The fire in my bones, the lion's embrace, the dreams of my godparents—all point to a God who is bigger than any boundary, who shows up in scripture, in Spirit, and in the wisdom of the earth itself.

Now the story shifts. In the chapters ahead, I step beyond the details of my own life into the deeper questions that have shaped it: What is gender? Did God intend the binary as we know it? How have culture, language, and power reshaped God's design? And most importantly—what would it look like to reclaim the truth that all humanity was created in the image of a God who is beyond gender?

PART II

The Unpacking: Theology, Gender, and Society

6

What Is Gender?

"There is neither Jew nor Greek, there is neither slave nor free, there is no male and female, for you are all one in Christ Jesus."
— Galatians 3:28*(NRSV)*

When I was growing up, no one separated the words *sex* and *gender.* They were used interchangeably, as if they meant the same thing. The doctor looked between your legs when you were born, declared "It's a boy!" or "It's a girl!" and from that moment, the rest of your life was scripted.

Girl: wear pink, be gentle, sit with your legs closed, prepare to be a wife and mother.

Boy: wear blue, be strong, don't cry, prepare to be a provider.

No one explained that *sex* refers to biological characteristics, while *gender* is a set of expectations, roles, and identities shaped by culture—not by chromosomes. No one told me that gender is a human language, not a divine decree.

My first lessons in gender came from home and church. In our strict Pentecostal household, I was taught that God had designed two fixed categories—male and female—and that my role as a "female" was divinely assigned. That meant dresses, long hair, no pants at church, no playing sports with the boys, and no imagining a future that didn't include marriage to a man.

At home, my mom enforced it with clothes and chores; at church, it was preached from the pulpit as "God's order." I learned quickly that deviation came at a cost: raised eyebrows, whispered gossip, and sometimes direct correction. Even when my mom eventually let me wear pants and play softball, I knew those freedoms were exceptions, not the rule.

And yet, deep inside, I felt an ongoing resistance. Not rebellion for rebellion's sake, but a quiet sense that something about this system didn't reflect the fullness of God. The Bible's first mention of gender appears in Genesis 1:27:

"So God created humankind in his image, in the image of God he created them; male and female he created them."

Most sermons I heard used this verse as proof of the gender binary. But when I began studying scripture for myself, I noticed something. The verse doesn't assign roles or hierarchy to "male" and "female." In fact, the blessing and commission in verse 28—"Be fruitful . . . and have dominion"—are given to both equally.

Carol Meyers, in *Discovering Eve*, points out that the Hebrew word for "human" (*adam*) originally wasn't a gendered term at all. It comes from the same root as "earth" (*adamah*), a reminder that we are formed from the ground itself. In other words, "Adam" first meant "earthling," not "man." Gender entered the story later.

Even in Genesis 5:1–2, the text says:

"When God created humankind, he made them in the likeness of God. Male and female he created them, and he blessed them and named them 'Humankind.'"

The emphasis is on the shared image and blessing, not on division.

From an indigenous lens, this makes perfect sense. Many First Nations, African, and Pacific Islander traditions teach that humanity's first identity is as *Earth-kin*. Before we are man or woman, we are children of the soil, born from Sky and Earth's union. In these traditions, gender is fluid and relational, more like seasons than cages—one may carry masculine energy in certain roles, feminine energy in others, and at times both or neither.

The balance of these energies is seen as sacred, necessary for community harmony.

If the creation story begins in equality and shared blessing, how did we end up here—with rigid hierarchies, cultural stereotypes, and exclusion?

Part of the answer is in Genesis 3. After the disobedience in the garden, God describes to Eve a life of pain and subordination: "*Your desire will be for your husband, and he will rule over you*" (Gen. 3:16). Many take this as a command, but it is actually a *consequence*—a description of what brokenness does to relationships, not a mandate for how they should be.

First, the grammar matters. In Hebrew, the verb is not in the imperative form (a command), but in the indicative (a statement of what will happen). God is describing the effects of disobedience, not issuing a divine order. It belongs with the other consequences listed: pain in childbirth, toil in farming, mortality in death. Just as thorns and thistles were not God's ideal for the land, domination was not God's ideal for human relationships.

Second, the context of Genesis 1–2 makes this clear.

At creation, both male and female are equally blessed and commissioned to have dominion (Gen. 1:27–28). The word for "helper" in Genesis 2:18 (*ezer*) does not imply subordination; in fact, the same word is used throughout the Old Testament to describe God as Israel's helper. Equality and partnership mark God's design. Subordination enters the story only after brokenness enters the world.

Finally, to read Genesis 3:16 as a mandate is to enshrine sin as sacred. If we say "God ordained men to rule over women" because of this verse, then we are sanctifying the curse instead of seeking God's redemption from it. The story of scripture is not about normalizing brokenness—it is about God undoing it.

Over centuries, that brokenness hardened into systems. In ancient Israel, a "whole body" was defined by male genitalia.

Anyone who didn't fit—women, eunuchs, intersex people—was often excluded from worship (Deut. 23:1).

Cultural value was tied to anatomy, not to the image of God.

The New Testament world wasn't much different. Roman and Greek society had strict roles for men and women, and early church communities often mirrored those structures. This is why Paul's statement in Galatians 3:28 was so radical: he declared that in Christ, those distinctions no longer determined worth or belonging.

For forty years, I lived as a woman in a society that told me my value depended on conformity. I wore what was expected, spoke how I was told, and played the role even when it fit like a pair of shoes a size too small.

From a metaphysical perspective, those years taught me about the Law of Correspondence—the idea that what is seen outwardly reflects an inward belief. I had been wearing not just ill-fitting clothes, but an ill-fitting belief about myself. Transitioning didn't erase my past—it reframed it. It was the conscious act of aligning the outer garment with the inner truth.

Living as a man has given me insights into how much of gender is simply performance. People treat me differently now—not because my essence has changed, but because they perceive me through a different lens. That shift has only confirmed for me that gender, as we practice it, is more about social agreement than divine truth.

When I look at Jesus, I see someone who constantly broke through the gender norms of his time. He spoke directly to women in public (John 4), welcomed them as disciples (Luke 8:1–3), received their leadership (Mary Magdalene proclaiming the resurrection), and treated them as theological equals. He also embraced eunuchs—people who, in his culture, didn't fit the male/female binary in socially acceptable ways. In Matthew 19:12, Jesus even acknowledges those "born eunuchs" alongside those who choose celibacy or are made eunuchs by others, refusing to shame them.

From both a metaphysical and indigenous view, Jesus was living in what many traditions call the *Two-Spirit* or *Whole-Spirit* way—the embodiment of all sacred energies without being bound by human categories. This is the way of healers, prophets, and wisdom-keepers across cultures: to carry both sun and moon, fire and water, in balance.

Metaphysically, gender is one of the many temporary conditions of earthly life. Spirit is beyond gender. The soul does not carry chromosomes. When Paul says in Galatians 3:28 that we are "one in Christ Jesus," he's pointing toward a spiritual reality that already exists: that in Spirit, there is no separation.

We are each a unique expression of the divine, and the divine contains all possibilities—masculine, feminine, and everything beyond and between. When we cling too tightly to gender as identity, we risk missing the greater truth: we are first and foremost Spirit, an emanation of Source.

Understanding the difference between sex and gender—and recognizing the cultural nature of gender roles—isn't just academic. It's liberating. It frees us to stop using gender as a measure of worth, authority, or calling.

If God's image is reflected in all of us, then leadership, love, and purpose cannot be restricted to one gender. The church's future depends on living into that reality, because God's Kingdom is not built on separation—it's built on unity in diversity.

Gender may describe aspects of our humanity, but it does not define the limits of God's image in us. The closer we come to living beyond those limits, the closer we step into the unity and freedom God intended from the very beginning—and the closer we align with the way of our ancestors, who knew that Spirit is whole, unbound, and infinitely creative.

7

Genesis Without Binaries

"In "So God created humankind in his image, in the image of God he created them; male and female he created them. God blessed them . . . "

— *Genesis 1:27–28(NRSV)*

When you've been taught a scripture one way your whole life, it's easy to believe that's the only way it can be read. Genesis 1:27 was one of those verses for me. I had heard it quoted as the ultimate proof text for a fixed, two-gender system—male and female, assigned at creation and sealed forever.

In Sunday school, the creation story was illustrated in crayon: Adam with short hair, Eve with long hair, both standing in a perfectly manicured garden. The teacher would point to the picture and say, "See? This is how God made it." That image became part of my spiritual DNA—not because it was necessarily true, but because no one offered me another possibility.

It wasn't until I began studying the Hebrew text that I noticed something that changed everything. The first human in Genesis is called adam, which doesn't mean "man" in the gendered sense. It means "human being" or "earthling," a creature formed from adamah—the ground.

Genesis 1 tells us God created Adam in the divine image, and then describes humanity as "male and female." But here's the detail we often overlook: the blessing comes before the division.

That order matters. God blesses Adam—humanity—first. Only afterward does the text name "male and female." This suggests that our deepest identity is not gendered; it is divine. The image of God is the root. Gender is a branch. When we reverse that—when we make gender the root—we distort the truth of creation.

From an indigenous perspective, this echoes the way many creation stories speak of humanity. Among several African and First Nations peoples, the first humans are not separated by gender but by purpose—each one carrying a balance of energies for the sake of the whole. In Yoruba cosmology, the orishas themselves embody multiple gendered expressions—Oshun's sweetness can also carry the ferocity of Ogun's strength; Obatala, often depicted as male, is also considered the gentle mother of all humanity. Wholeness comes not from division, but from integration.

Genesis 2 gives us a more intimate telling. God forms adam from dust, breathes life into the human, and places them in the garden. Seeing that "it is not good for the human to be alone," God decides to make a companion.

Many English translations say "helper suitable for him," but the Hebrew phrase is ezer kenegdo—literally, "a helper corresponding to him," an equal counterpart. The word ezer is almost always used in scripture to describe God as Israel's help, rescuer, or strength (see Psalm 33:20). It is a word of power, not subordination.

Yet somewhere in the retelling, helper was watered down to "assistant," and equal became "secondary." This misinterpretation transformed the story from one of mutuality to one of hierarchy. But the text itself offers no hint that one was to rule over the other—that only appears in Genesis 3, as a result of brokenness after the fall.

From a metaphysical standpoint, this is a story about consciousness before conditioning. The "blessing before division" reveals that our original spiritual identity exists whole and undivided, before we take on the labels and roles that the world uses to separate us. The "fall" is not just about sin—it's about moving from oneness into separation, from unity into the illusion of hierarchy.

If we strip away the layers of tradition, the creation stories in Genesis reveal a radically inclusive vision. In chapter 1, the image of God embraces male and female together, suggesting that neither alone reflects the whole picture. In chapter 2, relationship is built on equality, not dominance.

This is why Galatians 3:28 resonates so strongly with Genesis:

"There is neither Jew nor Greek, slave nor free, male nor female, for you are all one in Christ Jesus."

Paul isn't denying the reality of our bodies; he's saying those distinctions do not define our access to God, our calling, or our blessing. The same God who blessed humanity before naming gender in Genesis blesses the body of Christ before dividing it by category.

From a metaphysical perspective, this makes perfect sense. Spirit expresses through infinite forms. The divine image is not a fixed mold but an endless unfolding. Trying to limit God's creation to rigid binaries is like trying to pour the ocean into a thimble—it is not God's image that is too small; it is our vision.

From an indigenous worldview, the same truth is lived in the recognition of Two-Spirit and gender-diverse people as sacred. In many cultures, those who embody both masculine and feminine energies are honored as healers, mediators, and visionaries—because they reflect the fullness of creation in a single being. The ancient Hebrews may not have used that language, but the structure of Genesis points to the same reality: the image of God contains the whole, and humanity is blessed in its wholeness.

Spirit is beyond gender. The soul carries no chromosomes. In the eternal realm, identity is rooted in being, not in bodily classification. Gender may shape aspects of our human experience, but it cannot define the scope of God's image in us.

Understanding Genesis without binaries is not about erasing anyone's identity. It's about enlarging our theology to match the expansiveness of God's image. For some, that expansion will fit neatly into traditional categories. For others, it will not. But in both cases, the blessing stands.

When we make peace with a God who blesses before dividing, we can finally release the need to police identity, control bodies, or assign worth based on gender. The Kingdom Jesus announced is not built on separation—it is built on unity in diversity.

Once I began to see Genesis this way, I couldn't stop asking questions: If the opening chapters of scripture are more expansive than we've been told, how much of the rest of the Bible has been shaped—not just by translation—but by power? Peeling back those layers reveals the text as it was first spoken, first lived, and first imagined—not just in the Hebrew scrolls, but in the languages of the earth, the rivers, the wind, and the wisdom of the ancestors.

8

Power, Privilege, and Translation

"Do not conform to the pattern of this world, but be transformed by the renewing of your mind."
— Romans 12:2(NRSV)

Once you see Genesis without binaries, it changes how you read the rest of the Bible. You begin to notice how much of what we believe is shaped not only by the text itself but by the way it has been translated, interpreted, and preached.

We like to imagine the Bible as a direct, untouched word from heaven—as if God handed it down in English, leather-bound, with chapter and verse numbers neatly in place. But in reality, every Bible we hold is the result of human choices. Translation is never neutral. Each word is chosen by people—often people with power to protect, a worldview to defend, and a theological agenda to advance. Because human beings bring their cultural context with them, those choices shape theology for generations.

For most of Christian history, translators, theologians, and decision-makers were men from dominant cultural groups. Their readings reflected their priorities, their cultural assumptions, and their understanding of who should lead and who should follow.

Consider the shift from ha-adam in Genesis 1 to "Adam" as a proper name. In Hebrew, ha-adam means "the human"—a collective identity, not a male individual. But once it became "Adam," the first human became a singular male figure. That subtle change reoriented the story: the man is now first, and the woman is second. It's a reading perfectly suited to patriarchal structures—which is precisely why it endured.

Or take the Hebrew word ezer in Genesis 2. It's the same word used for God as Israel's strong helper and rescuer (Psalm 33:20; Deut. 33:26). But in many English Bibles, it is reduced to "helper" in the sense of "assistant," implying subordination. That wasn't inevitable—it was an interpretive choice. Once preachers repeated that word for centuries, it became "common sense" that women were created to assist, not to lead.

Power doesn't only shape the words—it determines which translations get printed, which footnotes get included, and which interpretations are deemed "sound doctrine." Over time, the theology these choices create becomes the air we breathe:

Junia, the woman Paul called "outstanding among the apostles" (Romans 16:7), becomes "Junias," a supposedly male name, in certain translations.

Phoebe, the deacon who carried Paul's letter to the Romans, is demoted to "servant."

Mary of Bethany, who assumed the posture of a rabbinic disciple at Jesus' feet, is reframed as a passive devotee rather than a theological equal.

These changes may seem small, but they are cumulative. They tilt the church's imagination toward male-centered leadership and away from the full, rich diversity of the early Christian movement.

This isn't just an academic problem—it's pastoral, emotional, and deeply personal. I've sat with women who were told they could never preach because "Adam was formed first." I've counseled couples who believed male authority in marriage was God's eternal will because they had never been shown Ephesians 5:21—"Submit to one another"—before the verse about wives.

I've prayed with LGBTQ+ believers convinced their very existence was incompatible with God's blessing because someone's reading of Genesis left no room for them in the image of God.

For trans people, the weight can be suffocating. I remember a young man coming to me in tears, believing he had to choose between his identity and his salvation. Together, we read Matthew 19, where Jesus speaks of eunuchs—some "born that way," some "made that way by others," and some who choose it for the kingdom of heaven. His face changed as he realized: there was no condemnation, no exclusion—only acknowledgment that human embodiment has always been diverse.

Even in my own life, I saw how gendered privilege operates. After I transitioned, I noticed people interrupted me less. My opinions carried more weight. My ideas were received without as much suspicion. I hadn't suddenly become wiser—what changed was how my voice was perceived now that it came from a "male" body.

That realization was sobering. If I now had access to credibility that had once been denied to me, I had a responsibility to use it for justice—to challenge the very systems that had once limited me.

Romans 12:2 warns us not to "conform to the pattern of this world." That command doesn't only apply to secular culture—it applies equally to religious systems that replicate worldly hierarchies and domination.

From a metaphysical standpoint, domination itself is a distortion of divine order. Spirit's authority is never based on anatomy, titles, or social privilege—it flows from alignment with truth. Translation, in this sense, becomes more than a linguistic exercise—it's a spiritual act. When we translate with integrity, we become co-creators in revealing God's vision of a Kingdom where no one is excluded from blessing because of human categories.

From an indigenous perspective, words are more than tools for communication—they are living forces. In many African and Native traditions, to speak is to create. Language is ceremony. The storyteller is not just retelling history; they are shaping reality. This means mistranslation is not simply "getting the word wrong"—it is altering the spiritual fabric of a people's understanding. Our ancestors knew that when you rename something, you can change how it is treated. The colonial renaming of people, lands, and rivers was not just a political act—it was a spiritual act of erasure. The same has happened in scripture when Junia becomes Junias, when adam becomes Adam, when Ezer becomes "assistant." The power of the original blessing is diminished, and hierarchy replaces harmony.

Once I began to see scripture through this lens, I could no longer return to the old patterns. But seeing the truth in the text was one thing—living it out in community was another. The real test came when my identity, my calling, and the church's expectations collided head-on. That's where the tensions truly began.

9

Living in the Tensions

"We are hard pressed on every side, but not crushed; perplexed, but not in despair . . . always carrying in the body the death of Jesus, so that the life of Jesus may also be revealed in our body."

— 2 Corinthians 4:8, 10(NRSV)

There is a unique strain that comes from living in two worlds that don't believe they can coexist.

On one side was my identity—my truth as a trans man, my lived experience, my embodiment of God's image. On the other was my calling—my responsibility as a pastor to shepherd, teach, and lead in communities shaped by a theology often hostile to people like me.

The place where those two met was not peaceful at first. It was a fault line. Some days I felt like a bridge, holding two shores together. Other days I felt like a rope in a tug-of-war—pulled by love for my community in one direction and the non-negotiable need to live authentically in the other.

The tension wasn't only internal. It showed up in how people responded after I came out and began my transition. Some in the church celebrated, telling me they saw a new freedom in my preaching and a deeper anointing in my ministry. Others avoided the subject entirely, treating my identity like a rumor they weren't sure they should believe.

A few were outright resistant, citing "God's order" and "biblical truth" as reasons they could no longer see me as a spiritual leader. One person said, "You can be a man out there in the world, but in God's house, you're still a woman." They didn't realize they were revealing something about their theology—that they believed God's image could be restricted by human categories.

This is where the tension sharpened for me. I knew my call had been confirmed long before I took testosterone or changed my name. I had been preaching the gospel, pastoring people, and ministering the Word while living under the label of "woman." If God had called me then—and I know God did—why would God revoke that call now that I was living in the truth of who I am?

Jeremiah's commission (Jer. 1:5) kept echoing: "Before I formed you in the womb, I knew you." God's knowing wasn't limited to my assigned gender or cultural expectations. God's knowing was of my whole self—body, soul, spirit—across time.
From a theological standpoint, the tension I felt was never between me and God. It was between me and the church's perception of God. The God I knew was not bound by human gender systems. But the church I loved had inherited—and defended—a theology shaped by those systems.

Choosing to live authentically meant accepting loss. Some friendships faded. Some ministry doors closed. Invitations to speak in certain pulpits stopped coming. And yet, new relationships formed and new spaces opened—spaces where my whole self was welcome, not just the parts that fit someone's comfort zone.

I often thought about Jesus' words in Mark 10:29–30, where he promises that those who leave houses, family, or fields for his sake will receive "a hundred times as much" in return-along with persecutions. I was living both parts of that verse: the loss and the abundance.

Living in the tensions has taught me that faith isn't about erasing the in-between spaces—it's about inhabiting them with integrity. Paul writes in 2 Corinthians 4 that we carry both death and life in our bodies. For me, that means acknowledging the grief of relationships that could not survive my truth, and the joy of relationships born because of it.

From a metaphysical perspective, tension is the birthplace of transformation. The in-between is holy ground. It is in the pulling, stretching, and resistance that new spiritual muscle forms. Tension is the Spirit's forge, where identity is tempered into something both authentic and unbreakable. It's where illusion is burned away so that the soul can remember its original shape.

From an indigenous perspective, this tension is the liminal space—the "betwixt and between" that many Native and African traditions recognize as sacred. In Yoruba cosmology, it is the crossroads, the place where Elegba stands, where choices are made and destinies are set in motion. In many First Nations teachings, it is the place between sunset and night, between ocean and shore—a space of deep spiritual power where transformation is possible. These spaces are not meant to be rushed through; they are meant to be honored.

I began to see my life not as torn between two worlds, but as standing in a sacred doorway. My role was not to resolve the tension but to live faithfully within it—holding the edges together until others could pass through.

hese tensions are not mine alone. Every LGBTQ+ believer in a faith community is navigating similar ground—living between personal truth and communal belonging, between God's affirmation and the church's hesitation.

The future health of the church depends on whether it can hold these tensions without breaking the people in them. Because when we cannot make space for the diversity God has created, we shrink the witness of the gospel.

By the time I began to embrace the tension as part of my calling rather than a threat to it, I was ready to step into deeper conversations—conversations about how the church's view of the Garden could be reimagined. If Genesis began with equality and unity, then perhaps the church could, too. That meant returning to the Garden with new eyes, carrying not just my theology, but also the wisdom of ancestors who have always known that life flourishes at the edges, in the in-between.

10

The Church I See

"See, I am doing a new thing! Now it springs up; do you not perceive it?"
— Isaiah 43:19(NRSV)

The tension I had carried for years was not just testing my resilience—it was forming a vision. What began as a personal ache for a place where I could belong has grown into a God-breathed picture of a community where no one is asked to choose between authenticity and belonging.

This vision is not hazy. I can smell the coffee brewing in the fellowship hall. I can hear laughter rising and overlapping in the sanctuary. I can see tears of joy rolling down the cheeks of someone who has been invisible for years, now realizing they are finally home.

I see a church where gender, sexuality, race, ability, culture, and history are not barriers to leadership but essential threads in the tapestry of God's image. Here, no one is "included" as an afterthought—they are recognized as vital from the very beginning. This is not tokenism. It is the original blessing of Genesis 1 brought to life: humanity declared "very good" before any divisions were named.

In this space, pulpits are shared by women, men, trans and nonbinary leaders, elders and youth. The sound of the Spirit's call is not filtered through human gatekeeping. Leadership flows from anointing, not from compliance with someone's checklist of gender, background, or appearance. Decisions are made at circles—not just tables—where every perspective is not only welcomed but needed, echoing Paul's vision in 1 Corinthians 12: the body cannot say to any part, "I have no need of you."

I see worship that tells the whole truth—songs from many cultures, prayers in many languages, testimonies from every corner of experience. This is the church of Pentecost in Acts 2, where the Spirit's arrival was not announced in one "holy language" but in the tongue each person could understand. The stories of those once pushed to the margins are not "special interest" moments—they are the heartbeat of the Gospel in action.

Our theology here loosens chains instead of tightening them. We open scripture with reverence and curiosity, refusing to treat it as a fossilized artifact. We acknowledge where human translation narrowed God's vision, and we reclaim the expansiveness that has always been present. Genesis becomes the story of blessing before division. Galatians 3 becomes a song of oneness without erasure. Romans becomes a witness to grace that outruns every boundary we try to draw. Revelation becomes a promise of a future where "every tribe and tongue and people and nation" stand together before the throne. In this space, scripture is not a weapon to wound but a wellspring to refresh.

From a metaphysical perspective, this church is a living field of consciousness—a collective soul space where Spirit recognizes itself in every face. It is the embodiment of John 8:32: "You will know the truth, and the truth will set you free." Truth here is not merely doctrine—it is alignment with the divine flow. When truth is lived, love becomes law, justice becomes rhythm, and authenticity becomes worship.

From an indigenous perspective, this church is not a building—it is a village. It is the sacred fire in the center of the people, tended by many hands. It is the talking circle where each voice is heard without interruption. It is the long table where the elders pass down wisdom and the children are invited to dream aloud. It is the drumbeat that calls us back into right relationship with each other, with the earth, and with Creator. Like the Ubuntu philosophy of Southern Africa, it lives by the truth: I am because we are.
And justice is not an occasional project here—it is the daily breath of the community. We do not stop at charity; we press into transformation. We don't just hand food to the hungry; we work to end the hunger itself. We don't just welcome queer and trans youth into the pews; we protect and affirm them in their schools, homes, and neighborhoods. Micah's call to "do justice, love mercy, and walk humbly with God" is not optional—it is our blueprint.

I know this kind of church will be called "too political" by some, "too progressive" by others. We will lose people who prefer comfort over transformation. But Isaiah's words burn in my heart: "See, I am doing a new thing!" This is not about erasing the old—it is about fulfilling what God has always desired: a people who live love as law, justice as rhythm, and authenticity as worship.

This vision is not mine to hoard. It is a shared calling meant to take form in real communities. My role is to speak what I see, live it where I can, and prepare the way for those who will carry it further. The tensions of my past taught me what was missing; the vision God has given me shows what is possible.
The only question left is not whether I can imagine it—it's whether we, together, have the courage to risk enough to see it come alive.

11

Vision in the Fire

"Write the vision; make it plain on tablets,
so he may run who reads it."
— *Habakkuk 2:2(NRSV)*

The vision came to me like light in a closed room—sudden, undeniable, illuminating everything it touched. In prayer, it was easy to believe. In worship, it was easy to proclaim. But visions are not meant to remain in safe places. Sooner or later, God calls you to walk them out where the air is thick with skepticism, the ground is uneven, and not every voice is cheering. In private, a vision feels like a gift. In public, it feels like a test.

When Habakkuk was told to write the vision, it wasn't so he could admire it in his personal journal—it was so "a herald may run with it." A vision is meant to be shared, carried, lived. But the moment you make a vision visible, it becomes vulnerable. It can be misunderstood, misrepresented, or resisted before it's ever embraced.

I started where I had both the most risk and the most responsibility: the pulpit. From the first Sunday after the vision took root, I felt the Spirit press me: Do not shrink the Gospel to fit the room. And I didn't.

I preached the whole counsel of God's welcome—justice and mercy, holiness and inclusion, truth and grace braided together like strands of a sacred cord. I preached women into the center of the Gospel story. I named queer and trans believers as beloved children of God—not as exceptions, but as part of God's family from before the foundation of the world.

Some sermons landed like fresh rain on thirsty soil. Others met the kind of silence that tells you old roots run deep. But the Gospel is not a guest—it does not wait for permission to enter. It is a kingdom that advances whether it is welcomed or resisted.

Like Jesus, I learned to weave truth into every message—sometimes openly, sometimes as parable—so the hungry would be fed and the powerful would be unsettled. Even those who thought they were coming to hear "something else" found themselves meeting the same reality: the reign of God that leaves no one outside the table.

But the vision could not stay trapped in Sunday sermons. It had to take form in the structure of the community. We reimagined leadership—not only who led, but how leadership worked. We began to break down hierarchies that concentrated decisions in the hands of a few and moved toward what Ephesians 4 describes—a body where each part functions in its gifting.

I sought the overlooked—the quiet leaders who didn't fit the mold. I invited the "maybe later" and "not yet" voices to step forward now. We prayed together, studied together, and learned to see ourselves in scripture without apology.

We also redefined success. Numbers still mattered, but they weren't the measure. The real questions became:

Are the marginalized becoming central?

Are the hesitant beginning to speak?

Are the young shaping the conversation?

Are the Spirit's gifts multiplying in unexpected places?

This wasn't glamorous work. Some days the vision blazed like fire; other days it felt like embers I had to shield from the wind. Bills still came. Schedules still clashed. Fear still whispered. But then there were the holy interruptions—a teenager declaring she wanted to preach, a first-time visitor whispering, "I didn't feel like I had to hide here."

From a metaphysical perspective, I began to see that this work was not building a structure—it was cultivating a vibration. The church was becoming a frequency of welcome, a resonance of truth, a place where the consciousness of oneness could be felt. Every act of justice, every word of inclusion, every shared table was a spiritual tuning fork, helping us align with the sound of God's kingdom.

From an indigenous perspective, I realized we were planting a village, not just a congregation. The vision was like tending a sacred fire in the center of the people—everyone's responsibility, everyone's warmth to share. Our decision-making began to resemble a council circle, where no one voice dominated and all were invited to speak. Like seeds sown in many directions, some took root quickly, others lay dormant until the season was right—but all belonged to the same planting.

And of course, there was resistance. From those who feared "too much change." From those who believed this space was "compromising the Gospel." And sometimes, from within myself—my own doubts about whether I was enough for this call.

But every time I thought of stepping back, the Spirit whispered the same thing: This is not your idea. This is My invitation.

So I kept walking. One sermon. One conversation. One open table at a time. Because visions may be conceived in prayer—but they are born in the fire. And fire, once lit, will spread if it is fed.

12

The Vision That Reshaped Me

"And we all, who with unveiled faces contemplate the Lord's glory, are being transformed into his image with ever-increasing glory . . . "

— 2 CORINTHIANS 3:18(NRSV)

I ONCE THOUGHT CARRYING a vision meant I was the one holding it. I would protect it, fight for it, and push it forward until it became reality. But somewhere along the way, I realized the truth—the vision was holding me.

It wasn't just shaping the church; it was shaping me. It was chiseling away the places I hid, softening the edges where I had grown too guarded, and strengthening my spine where I had been too quick to compromise. The same Spirit that gave the dream was using it as a mirror, showing me where my faith, my courage, and my authenticity still needed to grow.

In the indigenous way of knowing, a vision is not a possession—it is a living spirit that chooses you. Among many First Nations traditions, vision is understood as a sacred being that walks with you, teaches you, tests you, and shapes you until you are ready to live it fully. In African cosmology, a calling is not separate from the person—it is braided into your ori (divine head) before you are born, accompanied by the breath of the ancestors who agreed to walk with you. I was not just carrying this vision; it was carrying me through my own becoming. I expected the vision to change the congregation. I did not expect it to change me first.

In the beginning, I tried to lead from behind a protective wall. Share the dream. Inspire the people. Keep my personal wrestlings out of sight. But the Spirit kept pressing: You cannot call people into authenticity from behind a mask. Slowly, the work of creating a radically inclusive, Spirit-filled community began stripping away my own guardedness.

That meant confronting the subtle ways I still sought permission for what God had already authorized. It meant choosing to live fully in the open—not just as a trans man in ministry, but as a leader willing to lose the approval of the comfortable rather than betray the hope of the marginalized.

In indigenous tradition, a true leader is not the one who gathers the most followers but the one who can hold the fire without hoarding it—tending it so that others can take their flame and light their own paths. That truth humbled me.

I grew softer in compassion because I remembered how long it took me to unlearn what I had been taught. I grew stronger in conviction because I understood that protecting the vision sometimes meant saying "no"—even to people I loved—when their direction didn't align with God's call.

And in the space we were building, I met God in new ways. Not just as Provider or Protector, but as Co-Builder—shoulder to shoulder with me, sleeves rolled up, hands in the work. There were Sundays I could almost feel the divine smile: when worship erupted without a plan, when a testimony cracked open a heart, when someone realized they were fully seen and fully safe.

My preaching shifted. It became less about delivering polished conclusions and more about inviting people into the holy tension of seeking. The pulpit stopped being a stage for certainty and became a table for holy wrestling. There was freedom in saying, "I don't have all the answers, but I know the One who walks with us."

The vision became a mirror. It showed me where I was still managing other people's comfort instead of walking in God's freedom. It pulled me deeper into trust, deeper into courage, deeper into an unfiltered reflection of God's image in me.

From a metaphysical perspective, this was the law of correspondence in motion: as within, so without. The more I surrendered the false layers within myself, the more the external vision could expand. In the unseen, my consciousness was aligning with the frequency of the world I was called to build—and Spirit was matching that vibration with opportunity, provision, and people.

Theologically, I began to see this process through the lens of Paul's "from glory to glory" in 2 Corinthians 3:18. Transformation is not a one-time event—it's a continual unveiling. Every time I surrendered another fear, another hesitation, another false layer, the Spirit revealed more of who I truly was and more of what the vision could become.

And here's the truth: the vision God gave me was never just about the church's future—it was about mine. It was about learning to trust God as Co-Builder, not just as Architect. It was about recognizing that Kingdom change doesn't always roar in stadium revivals; sometimes it blooms quietly, in a teenager daring to say, "I want to preach someday," or a visitor whispering, "I didn't have to hide here."

In indigenous worldview, transformation is cyclical, not linear. You do not simply arrive—you circle back, each time at a deeper level of knowing, a fuller embodiment of your purpose. The elders say, "The path is made by walking it again." From that perspective, "from glory to glory" is not a straight climb upward but a spiral dance—returning to the same sacred truths with new wisdom each time.

In the end, the vision didn't just expand the church. It expanded me. It taught me that leadership is less about directing people where you want them to go, and more about walking with them into a future neither of you has fully seen. It taught me that God's glory isn't a static moment—it's an ever-increasing transformation, a deepening spiral that connects us to all who have walked before and all who will come after.

I am not the same man who first dared to say yes to this call. The vision I thought I was leading has been leading me all along. And I will follow it still—because every faithful step takes me, and takes us, from one unveiling to the next, from trust to trust, and always . . . from glory to glory.

Epilogue

Still Becoming—The Thread and the Circle

I HAVE LEARNED THAT vision doesn't end when you've named it, and transformation doesn't stop when you've embraced it. The work is still happening—in the sanctuary, in the streets, and in the hidden chambers of my own soul. Every day, I find myself becoming more of the person God called me to be, and every day the vision grows in ways I could not have imagined.

Looking back, I can see the thread that runs through every chapter of this journey, weaving grace into every turning point. In an indigenous way of seeing, this thread is not linear—it is a circle. Every ending folds back into a beginning, every revelation calls for new practice, and every transformation plants the seed for the next.

I learned that identity is not a burden to hide but a gift to embrace. Those first steps into truth taught me that authenticity is the doorway to freedom—and that walking through it often means leaving behind the safety of other people's expectations. Metaphysically, this is the work of aligning the outer life with the inner knowing, letting the Spirit that has always been within you finally radiate without obstruction.

I learned that the world will try to name you before you've named yourself, and sometimes the greatest act of faith is to speak your own name out loud and let it stand in the light. This is more than self-definition—it is sacred naming, the kind our ancestors practiced when they called forth the soul's purpose with every breath of your name.

I learned that faith is not static—it is alive, growing, and reshaping itself in the presence of God. The God I knew as a child stayed with me through every transition, widening my understanding of love until it could hold more than I thought possible. In indigenous teaching, the Creator's love is like a river—everflowing, carving new paths, yet always returning to the source.

I learned that inclusion is not a trend but a spiritual discipline. It is more than saying, You're welcome here. It is building a table where people know they were always meant to sit, where their stories are part of the foundation, not an afterthought. In the old ways, a feast was never complete if anyone in the village went unfed; wholeness was measured by the care given to the most vulnerable.

I learned that tension is not a sign of failure—it is the proof that transformation is underway. Seeds grow in the dark. Labor pains mean new life is on the way. Holy work will stretch you until you think you might break, but it is in the stretch that you discover a strength you did not know you carried. In the language of Spirit, this is initiation—the fire that tempers the vessel so it can carry greater light.

I learned that vision will shape you before you can shape it. You cannot call others into authenticity while hiding behind your own walls. The calling will pull you into deeper courage until your life and your message are indistinguishable from one another. This is the warrior's path in both sacred text and indigenous teaching—not the warrior who conquers, but the one who stands, unshaken, in service to the community. And I learned that the heart of the work is not about building bigger, louder, or faster—it is about building true. It is about faithfulness in the quiet seasons and trust in the One who can carry the vision further than you could ever take it alone.

In the end, the vision and I have become kin—each shaping the other, each calling the other deeper into what is possible. This is the circle I walk now: from glory to glory, from unveiling to unveiling, from one season of becoming to the next. And in the words of both my elders and my Spirit, I know this much to be true—this journey is not finished. It is only the next turn in the sacred spiral.

Closing Prayer & Blessing

Creator of Sky, Earth, and Waters,
You who breathe life into every direction—
East of new beginnings,
South of growth and fire,
West of endings and renewal,
North of wisdom and stillness—
we thank You.

We thank You for the ancestors who walked before us,
whose prayers became the path beneath our feet.
We thank You for the rivers that carry memory,
for the mountains that teach endurance,
for the wind that whispers truth when we grow weary.

Bless every reader of these words.
Let them hear the drumbeat of Spirit in their chest,
calling them back to themselves,
calling them back to the Great Belonging.
Let them know they are not alone—

the ancestors walk beside them,
the Earth holds them steady,
the sky reminds them of possibility.

Dismantle every chain that has kept them from dancing in their own skin.
Give them courage to speak their name into the circle without hesitation.
Give them tenderness for themselves and for others
as they do the holy work of becoming.
And when they are tired,
wrap them in the songs of those who prayed them into existence.

Now I speak this blessing over you:
May you walk in the freedom that can never be revoked.
May you stand in the truth that cannot be silenced.
May you live in the love that will never let you go.
May you rise with the sun,
root deep like the cedar,
flow strong like the river,
and carry the fire that will light the way for others.
And may you, too,
become a vision that reshapes the world.

Ase. Amen.

Appendix

The Language of Becoming

A REFLECTION ON THE WORDS THAT SHAPE OUR WHOLENESS

Every faith tradition has its sacred vocabulary—words that carry more than meaning; they carry memory. This "Language of Becoming" is not a dictionary but a devotional lexicon—each term a doorway into spiritual awareness, healing, and identity. These words have shaped my journey, rooted in Scripture, ancestral wisdom, and the metaphysical truth that God is alive in all things.

ADAM

In the Hebrew text, *adam* means "human" or "of the earth." It is not a name at first, but a description of origin—a being formed from the dust and breathed upon by God. Adam represents humanity in its wholeness: male and female, sacred and sentient, a reflection of divine image before division or hierarchy. To reclaim *adam* is to remember that our first identity was unity, not separation.

ANCESTRAL ENERGY

The living vibration of those who came before us—our bloodline and spiritual lineage intertwined. It is the unseen current that flows through our prayers, songs, and intuition. To honor ancestral energy is to recognize that we are the continuation of their dreams.

ANOINTING

The spiritual imprint of divine purpose. In biblical tradition, oil symbolized the setting apart of a person for sacred work. In lived experience, anointing is both gift and responsibility—the energy that empowers us to heal, teach, and transform.

BECOMING

The sacred process of unfolding into the fullness of who we are. It is both the journey and the destination, the healing and the revelation. To become is not to strive but to remember.

BELOVED COMMUNITY

A vision rooted in the teachings of Jesus and echoed through Dr. Martin Luther King Jr.—a world where love is justice embodied, and belonging is a divine right. Beloved Community is the manifestation of God's dream for humanity.

CALL / CALLING

The divine invitation to live one's truth in alignment with purpose. In Scripture, God's call was often met with resistance—yet always rooted in relationship. To answer the call is to say yes to becoming who you already are in Spirit.

COVENANT

A sacred promise between God and creation. It is not a contract, but a relationship—a mutual exchange of love, faithfulness, and trust. Each of us carries a personal covenant: the soul's agreement to walk in truth.

CREATION / CREATOR

The beginning and ongoing act of divine expression. Creation is not a moment in history but a continual unfolding of God through all things. To honor the Creator is to recognize that creativity is divine inheritance.

DIVINE ALIGNMENT

The moment when our inner truth matches divine intention. It is living in sync with Spirit's rhythm—where timing, purpose, and peace converge. Alignment is the yes beneath the surface of our being.

EZER

In Hebrew, *ezer* means "help" or "helper," but its true meaning is far deeper. It is the same word used to describe God as the helper and rescuer of Israel. Ezer denotes strength, power, and partnership—not subordination. To embody *ezer* is to stand as one who brings balance, restoration, and divine support into the world.

FAITH

Not certainty, but trust. Faith is the courage to walk even when the path is hidden—to believe that love will meet us on the other side of the unknown.

FREEDOM

The spiritual condition of being unbound. It is not merely political or social liberation, but the inward release from fear, shame, and limitation. In Christ's words, "Whom the Son sets free is free indeed."

GRACE

The unearned, unstoppable flow of divine love. Grace is not permission to avoid growth—it is the power that makes transformation possible. It is mercy meeting us where we are and calling us forward.

HOLY SPIRIT

The breath of God that animates all creation. The Spirit is not distant or abstract but intimate—our inner teacher, comforter, and guide. To live by the Spirit is to walk in awareness of divine presence in every moment.

IMAGE OF GOD (IMAGO DEI)

The truth that every human being reflects the divine nature. To be made in the image of God is to embody creativity, love, justice, and agency. It is the foundation of liberation—the sacred worth of all people.

INDIGENOUS WISDOM

The sacred knowledge rooted in earth, ancestors, and community. It teaches that everything is alive, connected, and communicative. To walk in indigenous wisdom is to live in right relationship with creation, Spirit, and self.

LIBERATION

The divine unbinding of the soul—from shame, oppression, fear, and every system that denies sacred worth. It is both spiritual and social, inward and outward, personal and collective. Liberation is love made public.

METAPHYSICAL

Beyond the physical; the study and awareness of what lies beneath appearance and beyond matter. In spiritual terms, it is the practice of seeing God in all things and all things in God. Metaphysical theology invites us to interpret Scripture symbolically, understanding that every story mirrors an inner truth. It teaches that transformation begins in consciousness before it manifests in form.

MORAL INJURY

The spiritual wound that occurs when one's deepest values are violated—by self, others, or systems. Healing moral injury requires compassion, truth-telling, and realignment with the soul's integrity. It is the labor of forgiveness and the work of wholeness.

PRAYER

The sacred conversation between the human and the divine. Prayer is not persuasion—it is participation in God's ongoing creation. Sometimes it sounds like silence, sometimes like tears, but always like truth.

RESURRECTION

The spiritual awakening that follows surrender. It is not limited to the body or to history—it is the daily rising of consciousness into love, courage, and freedom. Resurrection is the language of hope that refuses to die.

SACRED SPACE

A space—physical or spiritual—where the veil between human and divine feels thin. It can be a sanctuary, a song, a sunrise, or the stillness inside one's breath. Sacred space is less about location and more about awareness.

SALVATION

The ongoing process of becoming whole again. In Scripture, salvation means "to be made well" or "to be restored." It is not an escape from life, but a return to our divine essence.

SPIRIT

The divine essence that breathes through all creation. Spirit is movement, intuition, and revelation. To live in Spirit is to live awake—to see the divine in all things, including ourselves.

THEOLOGY

More than doctrine, theology is how we think and feel about God in light of our lived experience. It is the art of naming the divine through the lens of our stories. Liberative theology seeks not just to describe God, but to discover God within us.

WHOLENESS

The integration of our divine and human selves. It is not perfection but permission—to hold joy and grief, doubt and faith, shadow and light—without apology. Wholeness is the rhythm of a heart reconciled to itself and to God.

WORSHIP

The embodied expression of reverence and connection. It is not confined to a sanctuary or a song—it is the alignment of heart, mind, and action with divine purpose. True worship is not performance; it is presence.

These words form the rhythm and theology of Becoming Whole. May they serve as touchstones on your own path toward spiritual integration, liberation, and love. And may the God who holds all language remind you that the truest words are often lived, not spoken.

About the Author

AmunDayo (Khepra Oloririi) Edwards is a spiritual leader, teacher, and advocate committed to creating spaces of radical inclusion and deep transformation. He serves as the Master Servant of Integrated Praise Spiritual Center and the Executive Director of Integrated Praise Community Foundation (IPCF), a nonprofit organization dedicated to healing, empowering, and uplifting BIPOC TGI communities.

Through preaching, writing, and community building, he weaves together theology, lived experience, and a passion for justice to help others encounter the God beyond gender and binary limits. His ministry invites people to step fully into their truth, embrace divine diversity, and live as reflections of God's expansive image.

Bibliography

The Holy Bible, New Revised Standard Version Updated Edition. Nashville, TN: National Council of Churches, 2021.

Cone, James H. *The Cross and the Lynching Tree.* Maryknoll, NY: Orbis Books, 2011.

———. *God of the Oppressed.* Maryknoll, NY: Orbis Books, 1997.

Holmes, Ernest. *The Science of Mind.* New York: Tarcher/Putnam, 1998.

hooks, bell. *All About Love: New Visions.* New York: William Morrow, 2000.

Karenga, Maulana. *Maat, The Moral Ideal in Ancient Egypt: A Study in Classical African Ethics.* Los Angeles: University of Sankore Press, 2004.

Mbiti, John S. *African Religions and Philosophy.* Oxford: Heinemann, 1990.

Morrison, Toni. *Beloved.* New York: Vintage International, 2004.

Shange, Ntozake. *For Colored Girls Who Have Considered Suicide / When the Rainbow Is Enuf.* New York: Scribner, 1975.

Somé, Malidoma Patrice. *Of Water and the Spirit: Ritual, Magic, and Initiation in the Life of an African Shaman.* New York: Penguin, 1994.

Thurman, Howard. *Jesus and the Disinherited.* Boston: Beacon Press, 1996.

Tutu, Desmond. *No Future Without Forgiveness.* New York: Doubleday, 1999.

Vanzant, Iyanla. *Acts of Faith: Daily Meditations for People of Color.* New York: Simon & Schuster, 1993.

Walker, Alice. *In Search of Our Mothers' Gardens: Womanist Prose.* San Diego: Harcourt Brace Jovanovich, 1983.

Wilkerson, Isabel. *Caste: The Origins of Our Discontents.* New York: Random House, 2020.

www.ingramcontent.com/pod-product-compliance
Lightning Source LLC
LaVergne TN
LVHW020648100826
845148LV00012B/2373